Parenting a Struggling Reader

Parenting a Struggling Reader

Susan L. Hall

and Louisa C. Moats, Ed.D.

Broadway Books / New York

Broadway Books titles may be purchased for business or promotional use or for special sales. For information, please write to: Special Markets Department, Random House, Inc., 1540 Broadway, New York, NY 10036.

PRINTED IN THE UNITED STATES OF AMERICA

BROADWAY BOOKS and its logo, a letter B bisected on the diagonal, are trademarks of Broadway Books, a division of Random House, Inc.

Visit our website at www.broadwaybooks.com

Library of Congress Cataloging-in-Publication Data
Hall, Susan L. (Susan Long)
Parenting a struggling reader / Susan L. Hall and Louisa C. Moats.—1st ed.
p. cm.
Includes bibliographical references and index.
1. Reading—Remedial teaching. 2. Reading—Parent participation.
I. Moats, Louisa Cook. II. Title.

LB1050.5 .H26 2002
649'.58—dc21
2001046110

The authors discuss a variety of methodologies designed to aid struggling readers. Several of these contain trademarks or service marks. A list of these follows: Fast ForWord® • LANGUAGE!™ • Language Circle© • Lindamood® Auditory Conceptualization Test • Lindamood Phoneme Sequencing™ Program (LiPS™) • Lindamood-Bell™ • Lindamood-Bell Learning Processes™ • Project Read© • Reading Recovery® • Scientific Learning™ • Slingerland™ Institute for Literacy

FIRST EDITION

Designed by Fearn Cutler de Vicq

ISBN 0-7679-0776-0

7 9 10 8 6

To all the parents who have shared their stories with us, especially those who have allowed their quotes to appear in this book.

To my husband, David, a constant source of support and encouragement to "follow my passion." To my children, Brandon and Lauren, who provided the experiences that led me to my passion about children and reading.

—*Susan L. Hall*

In memory of my mother, Mildred Cook, whose unfailing curiosity about language, children, and teaching became my life's work.

—*Louisa C. Moats, Ed.D.*

Contents

Acknowledgments

We would like to acknowledge the time that several colleagues spent in reviewing sections of various chapters. Dr. Gordon Sherman reviewed the brain research section of Chapter 4. Joyce Pickering reviewed the description of the teaching approaches advocated by the International Multisensory Structured Language Education Council (IMSLEC) described in Chapter 7. And two lay advocates, Nancy James and Pat Howey, reviewed Chapter 9 to help us portray as accurately as possible an overview of the IEP process. Thank you, Gordon, Joyce, Nancy, and Pat.

Preface

I know firsthand the range of emotions a parent of a struggling reader can feel, because my child had trouble learning to read when he was in first grade. I share my story because it offers hope and encouragement to parents. Everything started out well for our son. His preschool teachers gave us nothing but positive feedback at each conference, as did his kindergarten teacher. His development, including speech development, was on track at each checkup with the pediatrician.

When our son was a preschooler, he loved to listen to stories read aloud to him. Because he was such an active boy, it always amazed me that he could be read to for an hour or more. We had done everything we knew (and were told) to do to prepare him for kindergarten. We had taught him the alphabet and had read, read, read aloud to him, not only every night before bed for fifteen minutes but also many times during the day. I can still retell some of his favorite stories such as the *Curious George* books and his preschool favorite, *Mike Mulligan and His Steam Shovel*.

When he started first grade, our son looked forward to school each morning. After school when he bounced out of the classroom to where I waited to walk him home, he would drag me by the hand back into the classroom to show me the spiderweb he had made that was suspended above his desk. As we walked home, he talked nonstop about his day, filling me in with rich details about what he had built in the block corner or the story the teacher had read to the class.

I noticed the first signs of change late in the fall. As he walked out of the classroom, his demeanor was subdued and he no longer wanted to show me anything. His enthusiasm was gone and he just wanted to get home as quickly as possible. On the way home when I asked my usual question, "How was school today?" he would say very little.

By January I knew something was wrong. Yet, when I asked my son questions, he didn't give me any information that pointed to what the problem was. When I received a phone call from a room mother asking me if I was available to help out in the classroom on a project, I jumped at the chance. I had to get into that classroom to try to figure out what was bothering my son. Why had he lost his enthusiasm for school?

On the designated day, I arrived in my son's classroom and was asked to work with a group composed of my son and four other children. Each child was to read a paragraph from a book the teacher had selected for our group. The other four children read before my son did, and I realized after listening to them that they read better than he did. When it was his turn, I watched his face as he read. His reading was slow and choppy. He stumbled over more words than the other children had, needed me to tell him nearly half the words, and reversed words such as *was* and *saw.* His face showed that he was sheepish and embarrassed. When I left the school building that day, I had a sinking feeling that we had a problem.

As I tucked him into bed that night, we talked about his feelings about his difficulty with reading. The memorable question my son asked me that night was, "Mom, why am I the first one done with the math sheets, yet I'm in the lowest reading group?" He knew that he was as capable as his peers but that reading was too difficult for him.

My first step was to ask his teacher whether she thought he was behind in reading. She had not mentioned any concerns at our fall conference. Until the day I helped out in class I really wasn't aware that he was in the lowest reading group. It had never occurred to me to ask that question at our parent/teacher conference. His teacher responded, "Don't worry. He'll catch up. It's just a developmental lag." She explained to me, "Children develop at their own pace, and some read earlier than others."

We continued to read aloud to our son every night. Since he needed a little extra help, I was prepared to spend some extra time listening to him read. But what I found was that he didn't want to read to me. When he did read, it was very laborious. He had to stop to figure out many words, sometimes hesitating so long that he lost track of the rest of a sentence. When he didn't recognize a word instantly, he would look around the page at the pictures and then guess the word. Often the word he guessed made sense contextually, but didn't even start with the same sound as the word in print. It was clear to me that he couldn't begin to sound out words.

As I watched how labored his reading was, I became increasingly worried. By March he was more discouraged than ever. Finally, I asked his teacher if he should be tested for a learning disability. I still remember her response. She said to me, "Oh no. I couldn't possibly refer him for testing. He's not a year behind." I remember walking out of that classroom very angry. All I could think about was that we were not going to wait for him to be a year behind before we figured out if he needed help. I was determined *not* to let him fail.

After repeated conversations with his teacher throughout the spring, we decided to have him privately tested. I didn't even really understand what a learning disability was, and I had no idea how to find someone to test my child. Someone we knew referred us to a psychologist, but he was not a very skilled or informed diagnostician. His report said that our son had a learning disability and an "auditory processing" problem, something the psychologist didn't explain very well when he met with us. And his advice was not very specific— just that our son would benefit from being taught to read with a phonics approach. He referred us to a learning clinic in a nearby suburb. When I called the clinic, however, they said they offered tutoring only to high school students. He also gave us a bleak picture about our son's chances of attending a good college.

This was the point when I began to network with other parents. I was amazed to find that many of my friends had experienced learning difficulties with their children. One of these friends referred me to her son's tutor, who reviewed our diagnostic report. She agreed that although the psychologist who had tested our son confirmed that he had a learning disability, he had stopped short of diagnosing a specific disability or proposing a plan of action to help. We hired another psychologist to do some more specific testing, but his only advice was to hire his wife as a tutor.

While we were having our son tested, he was also enrolled in a summer reading clinic at a nearby teachers' college. Although he wasn't making much progress in this clinic, a turning point in my journey occurred because of it. One day as I waited to pick him up, I saw a brochure about a master's-level workshop on the Orton-Gillingham approach. Since my friend's tutor had mentioned this approach, I enrolled in the workshop, which was taught by the president of the Illinois branch of the International Dyslexia Association. She gave me a list of six well-trained and experienced tutors, and by late August our son was seeing one of them, who was well trained in both the Orton-Gillingham and the Wilson approaches, two methods recognized by experts in the field. To become better informed, I began attending conferences sponsored by the International Dyslexia Association and other learning disability organizations.

With twice-weekly tutoring throughout second grade and half of third grade, he completely caught up to grade level in reading and has never slipped since. Today, he reads the same books as his classmates and scores in the 90th percentile in reading comprehension on standardized tests. He is a success story because of early and effective intervention. Although he is a terrific reader, he still has difficulty with spelling, written expression, and French.

Dyslexia is something you overcome; it doesn't just go away. Yet if only I had known six years ago that things would be going so well at this point, it would have helped me to overcome my fears and to know that the psychologist who originally tested him was simply uninformed.

Susan Hall

Introduction

When a child is struggling with reading, parents may experience a whole range of feelings, including helplessness, anger, inadequacy, and frustration. Parents tell us they feel as if they are lost in a complicated maze and cannot see clearly how to proceed. Many are overwhelmed with conflicting advice about what their child needs and are unable to sort out what to do and when to do it. Others feel angry that the school did not move quickly enough to help their child.

Parents often resolve their confusion and solve their child's reading difficulty through sheer determination, but many wish in retrospect they had had better guidance. Refusal to be deterred is a commendable quality, but parents should not have to make heroic efforts and experience repeated frustrations on the sometimes long journey to understanding the difficulty and finding help. Diagnosing your child's reading problem and getting the right kind of help does not have to be a bewildering and seemingly endless process. You can save valuable time, money, and emotional energy by following the advice in this book. Parents need not wend their way through the education maze alone.

Armed with good information, you can help your child read successfully. But only if you are informed can you make good decisions and advocate wisely on behalf of your child.

When teachers use research-based instructional approaches skillfully, nearly all children can be taught to read, spell, and write.

This book is unique because we have extensive experience working with parents who have sought help for their child's reading difficulty. I, Susan Hall, have experienced this journey firsthand with my child who had reading difficulties. My coauthor, Dr. Louisa Moats, is an expert in the field of reading and reading difficulties. Together we have listened to hundreds of parents tell their stories. The causes and cures for reading difficulties are well known in the research community, but classroom practice has been slow to recognize and use the information generated by research. Because parents expressed to us such profound need for straightforward guidance, we felt compelled to write this book.

When my own son experienced trouble learning to read and spell, I wandered through the maze of false starts and blind alleys for too long. Unfortunately, my experience is typical of many parents'. Most parents, like me, waste time and energy because of misguided advice and their own limited understanding of the problems their child faces. This book provides parents with advice and information, but most important, it provides hope.

We have organized the book around the questions and comments most often asked by parents whose children have trouble learning to read. Quotes from parents and teachers who have written to us on our website appear in shaded boxes throughout the book. The first section (Chapters 1–3) details the advocacy role that we recommend for you. It provides information about the major conclusions that have been drawn from scientific research on how children learn to read and what goes wrong for those who struggle with reading. The second section (Chapters 4–9) provides a detailed plan of action. This plan is divided into four steps:

1. Identifying a reading problem.
2. Having your child tested.
3. Seeking an accurate diagnosis.
4. Determining what instructional approach will be effective and how to recognize good reading instruction.

For more information, please visit our website at *www.proactiveparent.com.*

chapter 1

Parenting a Child
Who Struggles with Reading

> What a complicated maze it is trying to find accurate help for our children! My nine-year-old son is having difficulty with reading. He is in the third grade at a school where they are not at all concerned with his progress. My twenty-one-year-old daughter, who is in college, is also struggling. She attended Smith College for her freshman year, took two years off, and is currently at Colorado College as a struggling sophomore. It is sad to see such bright children work so hard and feel so bad about their capabilities. They echo one another in their personal commentaries about their perceived inadequacies. They say, "I'm stupid." "How come others can do it better? Read faster?"

This mother who wrote us expressed her frustration that children who are bright, eager, and well loved may find reading difficult. Their reality contrasts with a prevalent belief: that children learn to read naturally if their parents surround them with books from an early age. Who has not been told by a physician, teacher, or friend that if you read to your children from the time they are in the crib, they will grow up to be book lovers? You expect that normal, intelligent, book-fed children will take to reading as easily as they eventually take to bicycles.

Some do. Others don't. Unfortunately, only about 5 percent of children come into kindergarten having figured out reading, and 20 percent come to kindergarten knowing all their letters. By the time children leave kindergarten, about 17 percent will have significant difficulty with reading if they do not receive the right kind of teaching. The rest are likely to learn with an organized program, but how *well* and how *easily* they learn depend on what kind of program and how it is taught. Most children must be taught *how* to read, even though they love the books and stories the adults in their lives share with them.

Reading ability is like height and weight: it is distributed on a continuum. Some people are very good at it, some people are very poor at it, and the rest are somewhere in between. In this way, reading ability is like musical ability, athletic ability, artistic talent, and mathematical ability. Reading ability, however, is *not* just a reflection of intelligence. Some very intelligent children have trouble reading, and some decidedly unintelligent children can read fairly well. For children who have very few other problems, reading might not "click" and spelling might be well-nigh impossible.

We, the authors of this book, have bright children who experience difficulty with reading. Both of us have communicated with and worked with hundreds of other parents. We have learned that parents face unique problems as they seek help for a child who is struggling with words. When something as fundamental as reading is hard for one of your children, you may feel uncertain, anxious, confused, helpless, and—yes—angry if you cannot solve the problem easily. You begin to envision the worst. You acknowledge that this may be a challenging journey, for your child and for you, and that finding effective help may be no small task. One parent wrote this to us:

> I read your book *Straight Talk about Reading* and found myself getting angry. I was angry that I hadn't done more for my son who was still struggling with spelling. I was angry that I trusted the teacher to help with my son's spelling. But I did become convinced, after reading your book, I was on the right track having my son tested and having him tutored in the O-G [Orton-Gillingham] method. . . . Your story echoed "my son's story" almost exactly; however, I waited much longer than you to seek help for him. I believed the "developmental lag" theory I was being told by the first-grade teacher.

We receive many letters from parents. As they reflect on their quest for understanding and solutions, parents often share their regret over their inability to act sooner when they sensed that something was wrong. Many wish that they had known more about learning to read so that they could have made better choices or understood what their child was facing. The boy described in this letter did not catch up in his classroom even though his teacher believed that he would. Eventually, acting on her own, his mother arranged for him to be tested and to have individual, specialized instruction. In hindsight she wishes she had questioned the teacher's judgment and trusted her own. She wishes she could have saved her son a few days, months, or even years of anxiety about the written word.

Until the last few years, parent-friendly resources about learning to read and reading difficulty have been scarce. Now there are many websites, articles, and books for parents, such as those listed in this book. Most important, our recommendations are based on more than our collective experience. Scientists have generated enough research on how children learn to read, what causes reading difficulty, and what instructional methods work best with struggling readers so that you can avoid false starts and wrong turns in your search for help. But first let's examine why your role as the parent of a struggling reader presents some unique challenges.

Why is it hard for most parents to confront school personnel with questions about their child's well-being?

Reasons vary why parents of children with learning problems hesitate to question school personnel or express their concerns. Social rules, respect for the authority of teachers, and doubts about their own knowledge in a special area (e.g., reading instruction) inhibit parental action. Challenging school authority can be very uncomfortable for ordinary people. Many parents do not trust their own intuition about something as complex as teaching a child to read. Sometimes parents are simply reluctant to interfere too much in their child's life. They want their children to be independent and to manage school challenges without a lot of parental intrusion.

Enrolling your child in school assumes a tacit social bargain: the teachers will teach if you prepare your child to receive their instruction. Your job is to support learning from the sidelines. Indeed, research shows that children are more likely to succeed if their parents prepare them for school, provide good care after school, support homework, and encourage an interest in education. Teachers count on parents for home support and collaboration.

The tacit bargain assumes trust between home and school. With trust, you send your preschooler into the hands of receptive caretakers. With trust, you send your children to professionals whom you believe are trained to do a special job. With trust, you can overcome your natural tendency to hold on and be protective. You can reassure your child that school will be fun, interesting, and safe. You cheerfully conspire with teachers who help your child separate from you with as little fuss as possible.

Blind trust, however, can be hazardous. Although we want to believe that educators whom we trust should know how to meet our children's needs, time and again the parent is the first or only adult to recognize a child's learning problem. You, the parent, are first to notice the worrisome signs. Your child is complaining that he doesn't like school. At breakfast he reports a mysterious tummy ache or headache. When asked about his favorite part of the day, he says it's recess or lunch. He mentions his friends but not his schoolwork. He begs for you to continue reading aloud to him when many children are starting to read some of the words in books. He'd rather wash the dishes than sit down to read or write. When he finally does take out the book, he stumbles on every other word.

You know that something is amiss, but you get no validation from the school. You suspect that the other children in the class are learning more easily, but you have no way of being sure. You question whether learning to read should be this hard. If you are like many other parents, you ask the teacher's opinion. Your son's teacher says she does not think anything in particular is wrong and any day now your child will start to read. Dissatisfied, you want to ask more questions, but you don't know what to say. Doesn't the teacher know better than a nonprofessional parent?

All of our previous social learning does not prepare us to question the opinions or actions of well-meaning, dedicated teachers. Where are we trained to ask hard questions about how reading is taught, how progress is observed, and why our child might have difficulty? Nowhere. Yet the ability to ask these questions may be critical to the child's future.

Parents who question teachers or administrators may feel they are intruding or crossing an important role boundary. Teachers who must answer those questions may well feel that their territory is being breached. As with any employee in the workplace, teachers would like to have their judgment and expertise accepted. Many prefer to have visits announced ahead of time and are ill at ease if someone just "drops in" to see what is going on. This discomfort, too, is understandable: teaching is taxing, and justifying the curriculum is more than many teachers want to do. Yet the parent who is concerned about reading instruction *must* cross this territorial barrier in order to decide what and whom to trust.

Administrators may also give mixed messages about parental involvement in educational decision-making. They need parents for peripheral support, especially for raising funds and running extracurricular functions, but they want decisions about curriculum and instruction to reside with the professional staff. It is hard to run a school by yielding to multiple and sometimes ill-advised preferences of parents, and the professional staff works long and hard to choose how subjects will be taught. Parents usually have access to general information about standards, teaching approaches, and the curriculum but are seldom informed at the detailed level that is necessary to challenge reading instruction.

What approach to questioning the school do you recommend?

Assertive, respectful, and informed questioning is exactly what you need to do if your child is struggling with reading. Parents who want to become advocates for their child must distinguish between informed trust and blind trust and be willing to ask questions in areas traditionally "owned" by educators.

The most critical reason that you need to speak up and express your doubts, intuitions, or observations is that *time counts*. If there is one consistent message from reading research, it is that the earlier a problem is detected and treated, the more likely it is that the child will overcome it. Another reason is that there are teaching approaches and methods that work with most children who experience reading difficulty, and a change of approach may be needed. Once the child receives instruction using an approach that is systematic, intensive, sequential, and explicit, he may finally find the key to reading.

If I ask for the school to help and my child is labeled "learning-disabled," isn't this going to be a stigma that affects his self-esteem?

In 1999 the Coordinated Campaign for Learning Disabilities (CCLD), a consortium of six nonprofit organizations, commissioned a poll to examine the attitudes of parents about their child's learning problems and to assess the level of public awareness about learning disabilities. The poll revealed that the public is more knowledgeable about learning disabilities today than it was five years ago. More people realize, for example, that learning disabilities may affect specific academic skills like reading, and that the term is not another name for mental retardation. The public, however, does hold some harmful misconceptions about learning difficulties.

The most surprising outcome of this survey of seventeen hundred people was that parents wait a long time to seek help. The undue delay in seeking help often stems from their wish to avoid the stigma that they believe is attached to the label "learning disability." Nearly half of parents (48 percent) feel that having their child labeled "learning-disabled" is more harmful than struggling privately with an undiagnosed problem. The poll found that 4 in 10 parents have been anxious that their child might have a serious problem with learning or schoolwork. Yet 44 percent of these concerned parents waited for their child to exhibit signs of difficulty for a year or more before they acknowledged the problem. According to a news release by CCLD about the poll:

> Early identification of a learning difficulty often means the difference between success and failure for children struggling in school. Difficulties with basic reading and language skills are the most common learning disability—as many as 80 percent of students diagnosed with a learning disability have problems with reading. Apparently help by the first grade promises a normal reading ability for 90 percent of children with reading

disabilities. If help is delayed to age nine, 75 percent will have trouble throughout their school careers.

"It's clear from the poll that parents do not understand the importance of early intervention. With the right kind of help, children with learning disabilities can go on to be successful in their school careers," said Dr. Reid Lyon, Chief of the Child Development and Behavior Branch, National Institute of Child Health and Human Development at the National Institutes of Health. "But right now about 35 percent of children with learning disabilities drop out of high school. This is twice the rate of students without learning disabilities. Of those who do graduate, less than two percent attend a four-year college, despite the fact that many are above average in intelligence."[1]

You can read the entire report from the Roper Poll Survey commissioned by the Coordinated Campaign for Learning Disabilities on-line at:
www.ldonline.org/news/fact_sheet_may2000.html

Children have the best chance at success if the methods used at the outset teach critical skills. We can help older students to read and we do it all the time, but early intervention is best. The more time we waste in trying to figure out if there is a problem or waiting for the problem to cure itself, the greater the chance that the child will need more help later on. More help later on is difficult to come by and often very expensive. Parents who realize this know that they cannot afford to waste valuable time at the beginning *no matter what.*

The importance of acting on behalf of the child should outweigh reservations about the stigma of having a learning problem.

Your child's teacher may not be adequately trained to handle all reading difficulties, or may not have the support and resources necessary to help all children in her classroom. Many educators and psychologists do not have the training to understand and explain the nature of reading problems or to offer immediate and effective intervention that is grounded in research. Practically speaking, if your child's kindergarten, first-grade, or second-grade teacher is not experienced or trained to identify and instruct children with reading difficulties, then you may need to take matters into your own hands. The price of blind trust is just too high.

When my child is having a problem in learning to read, what is my role?

Defining your own role in addressing your child's learning problem can be tough. Accepting an active or assertive role might mean that the school's authority and control must be challenged. Yet you need to do so in a way that leads to an optimum solution for your child. We think there are several roles for parents that are healthy and that are likely to lead to better solutions to reading problems:

ROLE 1: Giving Emotional Support to the Child in a Time of Distress

Children who cannot read well may not be able to ask you directly for help, but they feel helpless. They may not know exactly what is happening to them, so they cannot articulate the problem for themselves, their teacher, or their family. They may feel lost in a large class and have trouble maintaining friendships. Listen carefully, watch closely, and help the child put his experiences into words. Let the child know you notice the problem and will work on solving it.

ROLE 2: Clarifying the Nature of the Problem

Your child's difficulties may emerge at home after the school day is over. Your child may show his frustration or skill deficits to you, while he masks them at school. You know your child well, and you have a special perspective to share with the teacher. Listen to your child's words and behavior, observe how he reads and writes, and share your observations.

ROLE 3: Pushing for Quick Action

Another critical role for you is advocacy when action should be taken quickly. If you feel a sense of urgency, that time cannot be wasted, by all means share it. Point out that delays put your child at greater risk in the long run. Monitor your child's reading progress and be willing to step in if your child gets off track. Do something as soon as you sense that his progress is not what it should be. Maintain your confidence that nearly all children learn to read with appropriate classroom and/or tutorial instruction. Keep pushing if the instruction is insufficient or you don't see signs of good progress.

ROLE 4: Gathering Additional Information

View the school as *one* of your information resources, not your *only* resource. Once you realize that you can use many sources of information to make sure that your child is getting a good reading education, you will be more confident. You can get credible, reliable advice from professionals, parents, and organizations. Whenever you disagree with the school's view of the problem or the amount of progress your child has made, seek an independent opinion. After all, in the health-care field we are encouraged to seek a second opinion.

You need to know enough about approaches to teaching reading to ask good questions. You need to know which parts of an instructional program are best supported by research, especially for children who struggle in learning to read. You need to know how the school determines when a child is behind and whether special services will be offered to help him catch up. Knowing your legal rights is also important so that your child will be offered what he truly needs, instead of the "boilerplate" approach that struggling readers often get (with unacceptable results).

Assessing whether the teacher or the school can teach your child to read may sound like a daunting task, but you make similar assessments all the time in your child's life. Most likely, you have already chosen child-care givers, physicians, and preschool environments that have been or will be good for your child. You chose a preschool using the same steps that you can follow in choosing a reading program.

Most likely, you visited classes, talked to other parents, and did some research on the differences between Montessori, private, and public programs. You can use the same techniques to assess your child's reading curriculum. You also need to trust your intuition about your child's well-being and be willing to invest the time and effort to find out about your options. One parent contacted us after receiving some advice she knew should be questioned:

> I have a five-year-old son who is not able to recognize letters or numbers despite our efforts. Our school district has evaluated both his sight and hearing and found them to be normal. Then they diagnosed him with ADD (no hyperactivity component). Now the school would like to send him to an ophthalmologist who specializes in dyslexia. Correct me if I'm wrong, but I was under the impression that dyslexia does not involve a visual deficit. The fact that these individuals have not remained up-to-date on the new research in this area deeply concerns me. I believe that we are at the point where we need to seek out an individual who specializes in dyslexia and can perform age-appropriate testing on him. But where do we start?

We do believe that parents should collaborate with school personnel as closely and as much as they can, and should give teachers a chance to demonstrate that they can meet a child's needs. For many reasons, you should exhaust all promising school resources, and then, if your concerns remain, you can seek outside advice and information. Actually, by seeking the expert opinion of someone outside the school, you are keeping the school on its toes. When parents are clear that they will bring in independent experts, school district personnel are likely to be more careful in formulating their opinions and offerings.

Your search for information and advice should focus on three things:

- Diagnosis—clarity on what the underlying problem is.
- Methodology—whether the services offered by the school are the most effective to solve the problem.
- Progress—whether enough progress is being made to get your child back on track as soon as possible.

Sometimes the methods the school is using to teach your child to read are known to be less effective than another approach or program. At other times, the methodology could be sound, but the teacher may not have the training, time, resources, or supervision to deliver it effectively. Sometimes the methodology is right and the teacher is excellent, but the intensity of the instruction is not enough. Many parents decide that the most efficient and effective way to help their child is to hire a private reading tutor to work with the child outside of school or to attempt home schooling with a program the parents purchase on their own.

But wait, you are likely to say. Why is all this up to me? Why should I have to hire outside tutors to do what the school should be doing? Many parents expend a lot of emotional energy dealing with this question. We will discuss this complex issue later in the book. One reason why many parents are thrown back on their own resources is that the school is not required by law to offer the best available services. They are obligated to ensure that a child derives "educational benefit," a term that is poorly defined and that often does not translate into "the program most likely to get the best results."

Determining whether the methodology the school is using to teach reading is right for your child may seem difficult. It is easier than you think once you are well informed. In

Chapter 2 we will provide an overview of research findings about reading development and science-based strategies that are most effective in teaching children to read. Although delivery of excellent reading instruction requires a well-trained teacher, recognizing whether a teacher uses a science-based approach is not too difficult if you know what you're looking for. As a parent you do *not* need to know how to teach reading—just how to evaluate what approach your child's teacher is using and whether it is working for him.

Your job is more clear-cut if your child isn't making any progress with the reading help the school is offering. That, however, is rarely the case. What is more difficult, and almost always the case, is that your child is making *some* progress but you are not sure if it is enough. Is it as much progress as the child could be making with a different approach or with a different instructor? Will it get him caught up to grade level as fast as possible? Are we doing the best we can do for him? Since these are tough judgments, you will most likely need to find experts who can help answer these questions.

ROLE 5: Advocating for Your Child and for Change That Helps Other Children

Many school systems that have strong leadership will offer what they believe is the best available approach within their budget constraints, but you may be able to push them to offer what is truly optimal instruction. Most teachers want to use the best available approaches; they are sometimes misinformed as to what those are, however, or inadequately trained to implement them.

Even if you are in good hands, you should become an advocate simply because your child is too young to advocate for himself. You need to listen to your child, bring all your observation skills to the challenge, and speak on his behalf. It is our experience that children with reading problems who ultimately catch up to grade level often have at least one parent who played a major role in this success story.

You need to remember that school personnel are responsible for balancing the needs of all the children in the school. You are the only one who can focus entirely on your own child and advocate for what he needs without bearing the responsibility for many other things simultaneously. Because the school personnel cannot legally advocate for your child, you sometimes need to hire or otherwise obtain outside experts to work on behalf of him. These experts are not employees of the school district, as the school psychologist and your child's teachers are.

Your sense of urgency can help your child's needs be met swiftly and satisfactorily. Hearing other parents' stories of waiting and living with the consequences of delayed action is usually enough to convince a worried parent to begin his or her own process of becoming informed.

Why is it so important to be informed?

The informed consumer makes better choices. Most people research major purchases before they commit to them. The more time you spend researching car safety records and customer satisfaction surveys of previous buyers, the more likely it is that you will make a good decision when you purchase a new vehicle. The same care can be taken in evaluating a program of reading instruction.

Making informed choices takes time up front but will save

time in the end. Parents who rely on casual referrals, or who rely on a professional without critically evaluating his or her credentials, may be buying trouble. Valuable time can be wasted if an uninformed professional gives you an incomplete or inaccurate assessment or recommends an unqualified tutor instead of a certified, trained therapist. Having to change programs, teachers, or tutors almost always involves more lost time for the child, even though the better results may justify a change in the long run. Some research and planning on your part can bring stability to a child who needs to settle in and get down to work.

I (Susan) watched a family in our community lose valuable time when they chose the wrong person to tutor their child. The mother had great intentions but simply did not take the time to become informed. I knew this family because our children had been in the same kindergarten and first-grade classes, and they had played together outside of school. The little girl was a bright, articulate child whom I observed eagerly participating in class discussions on the days when I was in the classroom as a mother helper.

My son and my friend's daughter were having trouble learning to read in first grade. We shared that common problem, but our approaches to dealing with the problem took completely different paths. When our son first had difficulty in learning to read, my husband and I went to great lengths to determine why he wasn't learning to read with the approach his teacher was using. We asked the teacher for help and advice first. But when her advice did not make sense to us, we began researching on our own until we got answers that did make sense. Our journey finally led us to conclude that our son needed a multisensory systematic phonics approach. It led us to reliable sources for tutor referrals, and after interviewing six tutors, we confidently selected the one that ultimately taught our son to read.

At about the same time that our son began his tutoring, our acquaintances began their journey by relying solely upon their daughter's teacher for advice and help. The mother expressed her concerns to the teacher and then hired that teacher to tutor the child after school. In the spring of our children's second-grade year, the mother wanted to know the name of our son's tutor because she was aware that our son was making considerable progress. She hired the tutor, Mrs. D., to work with her daughter once a week, while the child continued being tutored by the classroom teacher a second hour each week. The mother did not want the teacher to know that she had hired an outside tutor. After about two months of working with our tutor, the daughter told her mother, "Gee, Mom, Mrs. D. could sure teach Mrs. G. [her classroom teacher] a lot about teaching reading!" Once she began to make real progress in learning to read, even the child knew the difference between effective and ineffective teaching.

We recommend that you invest a little time in learning about reading instruction so that you are ready to make good decisions. You need to know:

- What scientific research says about good reading instruction.
- How to tell if your child's teacher uses "best practices" reading instruction.
- Why teachers are not always informed about reading difficulties.

- When to know that your child's difficulties require attention.
- How to explore getting your child help through school.
- How to use the legal system to get the best help for your child.
- When it's time to get an independent opinion (outside the school).
- What sources of information are most reliable.
- When it's time for testing.
- How to find someone to test your child.
- How to find a qualified tutor or educational therapist.

All of these topics are covered in this book. The next few chapters focus on the importance of being informed and why you are your child's best advocate. Then we provide a four-step process that starts with getting your child tested and concludes with determining the best plan for teaching your child to read successfully.

chapter 2

The Importance of Being Informed

My daughter is in kindergarten and has been recommended for a transitional first-grade program (two-year first grade). Her kindergarten teacher used the whole language approach, and my daughter does not know how to sound out words. She has lost confidence in herself because she cannot read and she sees others in her class who do. Fortunately, the T-1 (transition—first grade) teacher teaches phonics, because she does not believe in the whole language approach. However, she seems to be in the minority. Also, the school district, as part of the expense-cutting, budgeting process, seems to be set to cut and/or eliminate programs that target "at-risk" elementary-age schoolchildren. I know that my husband and I have our work cut out for us to ensure that our daughter is successful in school. Our experience has shown us that parents really do need to do a lot of research and be their child's advocate.

We couldn't agree more with this mother's concluding statement: parents who become concerned about their child's reading *do* need to do some research and become their child's advocate. This parent knows that her child is falling behind in reading. Although she is no education expert, she can tell that the approach used by her daughter's kindergarten teacher wasn't effective. It may have worked satisfactorily for other children, but it did not for her daughter, who is not prepared to read. While this mother is encouraged that her daughter's next teacher uses a phonics approach, she realizes that she and her husband will have to be *informed* advocates. These parents know that they, more than anyone else, have their child's best interests in mind.

In order to ensure that your child's reading development is on track, you need to know how to tell if your child is falling behind in reading, and you need to be able to recognize effective reading instruction. The first step in becoming informed is to understand the main findings of scientific research about reading instruction. Over the past two or three decades an enormous amount of progress has been made in understanding the following:

- What an efficient reader does while reading.
- What types of instruction are most likely to assure that the greatest number of children from all backgrounds will be successful in learning to read.
- How many children struggle in learning to read.
- What causes reading difficulty.
- What can be done to minimize reading difficulties.

In this chapter we explain the findings of research in laypersons' terms, define whole language and systematic phonics, and describe what effective reading instruction looks like. But first we need to discuss why reading instruction has become so controversial. Even parents whose children don't struggle in learning to read need to monitor overall reading achievement levels in the schools and become actively involved in advocating for change where scores are low or declining.

Why have reading scores declined in many states and districts?

Reading achievement has not improved across the nation for several decades and has actually declined in many states and school systems. Determining exactly where our nation is in reading achievement has been a challenge because we have no national testing program in the United States. We do have a voluntary testing program, the National Assessment of Educational Progress (NAEP), in which about three-quarters of the states participate. It is the only standardized test that provides data about changes in achievement levels in our country over time, and the performance of students in one state in comparison to that of another. In the thirty-six states that participated in the NAEP testing program in 2000, 38 percent of all children in fourth grade read below the basic level for their grade.[1] This finding is stable; overall reading achievement is not getting better. Of even more concern is the fact that in many urban, poor, minority school districts, the rate of reading failure is 70 to 80 percent.

One of the most interesting stories told by the NAEP scores occurred in California. After a decade of state-sponsored whole language instruction, California's 1995 NAEP scores fell to a tie with Louisiana for the worst achievement scores in the nation, down from a middle-of-the-country ranking a decade earlier. Education decisions in California are centralized, unlike the practice in most states, where decisions about what and how to teach are made on a district-by-district, and sometimes school-by-school, basis. The California Department of Education determines the standards and teaching approaches that will be used, and rewards schools that comply with the guidelines. Therefore, when the Department of Education discouraged the teaching of phonics, spelling, grammar, and other skills, endorsing instead the whole language approach, the reason for declining student achievement was obvious.

After an outpouring of concern by Californians in 1995, the Department of Education and the legislature designed and funded a series of initiatives to improve reading instruction. The embarrassment of achievement declines spurred those responsible for California's schools to look at scientific studies and seek advice from leading national experts. Every aspect of reading education in California was changed by more than a dozen pieces of legislation in an effort to promote instructional approaches that had been proved effective. The California Department of Education then sponsored a rewrite of the state achievement standards. These standards are regarded as some of the best in the nation, especially in early reading instruction. They specify that all components of reading must be taught, including phonological awareness, spelling, word recognition and phonics, vocabulary, comprehension, grammar, writing, and literature appreciation.

There are many initiatives under way in California today to implement better reading instruction in the schools. The David and Lucille Packard Foundation has funded the Reading Lions Project, which now has about thirty participating school districts, including Sacramento Unified and Los Angeles Unified. The Reading Lions Project supports the adoption of a phonics-based, comprehensive reading program called Open Court Reading, published by SRA/McGraw-Hill. In addition, there are reading coaches in each school and a detailed assessment program that helps teachers know if children are learning.

The program is comprehensive but structured; it contains teacher guides that are very explicit on how to teach phonemic awareness, phonics, and comprehension strategies. Included with the classroom curriculum is a set of books that students read in class, with copies to take home. These early books contain a high percentage of words that can be sounded out with the skills that have been taught and practiced in class, often referred to as "decodable" books. One of the key components of the Reading Lions Project is intensive professional development, especially for the reading coaches. Teachers receive instruction and practice in how to teach children to hear and blend speech sounds, expand sentences, summarize main ideas, and so on.

Many people in California believe that an entire generation of children missed out on good reading instruction and therefore have not developed skills in reading and spelling that are as strong as they might be. Of even greater concern is that California was not alone; many other states have been adversely affected by the popularity of whole language ideas. Whole language still affects what is taught today, although the ideas have been vigorously challenged and successfully replaced in many classrooms. Many states have recently launched major reading initiatives to improve reading achievement. Early intervention to prevent reading difficulties is one of President Bush's top priorities.

What is the whole language approach?

Whole language is an approach to teaching reading that is based on a belief that children learn to read by surrounding them with good literature and emphasizing the meaning and purpose of reading. One of the fundamental principles of the whole language approach is that children learn to read as "naturally" as they learn to talk. Children learn to talk through exposure to speech. Whole language advocates believe that teaching the component skills of reading in isolation, out of the context of sentences or passages, may damage a child's love of reading. This belief leads teachers to teach reading by encouraging children to recognize whole words by sight, instead of teaching them the sound associated with each letter. Whole language teachers have children follow along as they read "big books" several times until the words are memorized.[2]

One of the consequences of the shift to whole language was that many school districts abandoned commercially available reading programs in favor of teacher-made curriculums and programs. Teachers created their own reading curriculums because the central material needed was "authentic" children's literature. Money available for reading was shifted from traditional basal reading programs (workbooks, spelling books, decodable stories for the children to read, teachers' guides with phonics lessons) to the purchase of multiple copies of paperback books of "authentic" literature for the classroom—the same books that you would buy in the children's section of a bookstore. Eventually, the publishing companies began assembling kits with multiple copies of paperbacks and a large "big book" copy for the teacher to use with the whole class, but the information in the teachers' guide about direct instruction in the precursor skills of reading was gone.

Of course, few people would disagree about the importance of great books and fine literature in the reading program. But it's how the literature is used that is the issue. Most of the paperback books that we see in whole language first-grade classrooms are attractive and colorful with interesting stories, but they are filled with words that emerging readers have not been taught the skills to sound out. Instead, students are encouraged to decipher unknown words by guessing a word that would make sense, looking at the pictures for cues, looking at the beginning sound, or skipping over the words until they have finished a sentence. When children who are just beginning to read are given books with words that they cannot sound out, the message they receive is that they are supposed to guess at words, a habit that is not recommended by the scientific research. A parent wrote about practices that her child's teacher encourages:

I discovered how far behind my daughter was in first grade when I helped out in the classroom one day and the teacher asked me to give spelling tests. Several of her friends could sound out words as they spelled. My daughter couldn't sound out two letters, let alone seven. The teacher maintained that these spelling words came from stories in her Language Arts textbook and that the pictures would give her the "associations" she needed to recall the specific order of the letters. One lesson included the words *red, green, watermelon,* and *apple.* With or without the pictures, my daughter was clueless. The phonics lessons that were taught were unconnected to what she was reading and because she couldn't sound out words, the lessons were ineffective anyway. The teacher said to me, "One day it will just click for her. You'll see." Of course, it didn't.

When this parent was told that her daughter would figure out the words from making "associations" from the pictures, this was an ineffective instructional practice. Recent consensus papers on reading research agree that the most effective practice is to teach children to sound out words.[3] The context mainly helps children decipher word meanings once they have been correctly pronounced. Controlled studies of good readers show that they can guess only 10 to 25 percent of words correctly from context.[4] Even if a child is good at guessing from clues, once a child reaches fifth grade, the pictures are gone and the introduction of new and harder vocabulary accelerates. Skipping a word can interfere with getting the meaning of the text. Often the word that was skipped is a new content word—it contains the most critical part of the meaning of the entire sentence.

Research also shows that the most skilled readers are efficient at reading single words and that they rely very little on context for figuring out unknown words. Although skilled readers may appear to skip words, studies tracking eye movements confirm that good readers read every word and are processing the print letter by letter. Thus, skilled readers see all the letters in each word; they miss very little even though perception and interpretation of print occurs quickly and unconsciously. Skilled readers also become efficient at recognizing common letter patterns. After several exposures to a new word, the skilled reader builds a habit that is referred to as "reading by sight." She is able to recognize familiar words without being aware of the letter-sound association. In learning a new word, the average young reader will need to "see" and "hear" all the parts until they can be processed in larger chunks and recognition patterns are established.

Ineffective Practices for Figuring Out an Unknown Word

- Guessing based on the first letter of the word.
- Guessing based on the pictures.
- Skipping the unknown word and reading on to use context clues to guess.

Now that there is a research consensus about how to teach reading, commercial reading programs are changing dramatically and quickly. By the fall of 2001, all major publishers that sell materials in California had to design them with direct instruction in phonemic awareness, phonics, reading fluency, spelling, comprehension strategies, and other reading skills. Some teachers have welcomed this change because the whole language method was not effective for many of the children in their class. Others are angry that they have lost some control over their own classroom curriculum.

Does a whole language teacher teach any phonics?

The whole language approach and a systematic phonics approach should not be differentiated on the basis of whether *any* phonics is taught, but rather how much phonics is taught and how and when it is taught. Phonics is the system by which letters represent sounds. A whole language teacher wrote a message to us on our website on this topic.

She wanted to let us know that it is often stated that "whole language does not use explicit phonics instruction, and that is untrue." She continued by making the point that whole language teachers often read a story, then teach an explicit phonics or skill lesson "from the literature that was just read," and then the class turns back to the story. She said that "teaching skills in isolation is a practice that whole language teachers don't support."

The rationale sounds very compelling, doesn't it? Yet parents need to be wary of arguments such as this one. First, these ideas have been repeatedly tested in systematic, controlled comparisons of methods and found to be less effective than direct phonics instruction that is planned ahead of time. Second, when a teacher relies on teaching skills only when the need arises out of reading a story, she is much less likely to cover all needed skills in an order that logically progresses from simple to complex. Too often the timing of the phonics lesson is dictated by the particular choice of book for that day. The opportunistic "minilesson" on a word pattern or sound-letter correspondence may not present information in an order that helps children learn it. New concepts are presented to children too fast and with insufficient building of one skill on another. Whole language seldom provides enough practice of that day's lesson, let alone practice of what has already been taught. This is very different from a systematic phonics approach where the order of teaching all the sound-letter correspondences is determined in advance, and the literature for the day is designed to give the student practice in what she has already been taught.

The most recent and comprehensive review of reading instruction research was conducted by the National Reading Panel in April of 2000. The panel's report was commissioned by Congress. The following excerpt from the National Reading Panel's report *Teaching Children to Read* provides more guidance on the practices that differentiate the phonics taught in whole language instruction from the systematic phonics that is recommended by the scientific research:

Although some phonics is included in whole language instruction, important differences have been observed distinguishing this approach from systematic phonics approaches. In several vignettes portraying phonics instruction in whole language contexts, few if any instances of vowel instruction were found. This contrasts with systematic phonics programs where the teaching of vowels is central and is considered essential for enabling children to decode. Another practice that is found in some systematic phonics programs but is not found in whole language programs is that of teaching children to say the sounds of letters and blend them to decode unfamiliar words. Programs that teach this procedure are referred to as synthetic phonics programs. Systematic phonics programs also commonly teach children an extensive, pre-specified set of letter-sound correspondences or phonograms while whole language programs teach a more limited set, in context, as needed. Systematic phonics programs teach phonics explicitly by delineating a planned, sequential set of phonic elements and teaching these elements explicitly and systematically; some systematic phonics programs also use controlled vocabulary (decodable text) to provide practice with these elements. Whole language programs do not pre-specify the relations to be taught. It is presumed that exposing children to letter-sound relations as they read text will foster incidental learning of the relations they need to develop as readers.[5]

What does it mean when my child's teacher says that she teaches a "balanced approach"?

There is no way to know what someone means by this term. Most teachers use an approach that is neither pure whole language nor pure phonics, but some mixture of the two. The new buzzword is "balanced" reading curriculum, although we fear that this term can be as misleading as many other terms have been. In an effort to please questioning parents, many teachers are now claiming that they teach a balanced reading curriculum, which implies that they teach a combination of techniques from whole language and phonics. As appealing as "balanced" sounds, many educators who say their curriculum is balanced are no closer to teaching what research recommends than if they taught the whole language approach.

The research community has moved way beyond thinking

of this as a debate between phonics and whole language. Researchers are focused on defining exactly what skills a child must possess in order to read well and what classroom instructional practices produce the best results for the most children. For starters, we know that a child's oral vocabulary, familiarity with books, and general language comprehension will eventually be important for comprehending the more formal language in books. Next, children must develop awareness of the speech sounds in words in order to match written symbols (letters) to those sounds. We now know what to expect of young children, how to screen them for this type of speech sound awareness, and what to do when they fall short of the desirable benchmark. The focus of research now is on defining what kind and quality of instruction should be given at what level of intensity, for what duration, to which children, and at what point in their reading development. Some good answers to parts of this question are already available.

Parents need to know what scientific evidence says about good reading methodology and how to recognize it in a classroom. Hearing a term like "whole language," "balanced," or "phonics" really isn't going to tell you enough of what you need to know to evaluate your child's curriculum. You need to look beyond the terms and know how to recognize good instruction when you see it. To help you do that, in Chapter 7 we give you a description of a day in a kindergarten classroom and a first-grade classroom that use good instructional practices.

For now it is sufficient to understand that children who are successful in reading have learned how to read single words completely, accurately, and fluently. Some children learn this relatively easily and seem to read effortlessly. Many others must be explicitly taught through a structured process in which they are first made aware of sounds and the letter symbols that represent them. In addition, the instruction in sounds and letters must be followed by lessons that teach children to blend these sounds into words. The patterns of print must be noticed, understood, and processed fluently. Once children achieve accuracy in word reading, they can pick up fluency through much reading practice and some special techniques we will discuss later. From the beginning, comprehension should be taught, first by teachers talking about their own thought process while stories are read aloud to the class. After the child begins to read to herself, she can apply the same thought processes that were encouraged during read-aloud time. All of these components are included in a reading program that is truly balanced.

Aren't teachers held accountable for using research-based teaching practices?

I started teaching third grade in 1988, the last year that direct phonics instruction was used in our school district. Although I didn't know the jargon, I basically believed that children learned to read by reading and welcomed the "literature-based" approach, which was actually whole language. Within three years I could see that children arriving in third grade could no longer read nearly as well as their predecessors had. I now realize that whole language was a dismal failure. I was one of those teachers who was never taught how to teach reading, so

I've had to pick it up myself. In fact, at one of our district's professional development workshops a presenter who still believes in whole language recently said, "Phonics is like hair oil. All you need is a teeny-weeny bit." How can these people be approved by the state?

Until recently, public schooling has been lacking in accountability. Educators have chosen to use ineffective teaching practices even when the scientific evidence shows that other practices are better. Over the past fifty years, the predominant method to teach beginning reading has swung like a pendulum between approaches that teach skills and approaches like whole language that deemphasize the explicit teaching of skills. The National Reading Panel noted the instability in teaching practices:

When today's educators discuss the ingredients of effective programs to teach children to read, phonemic awareness receives much attention. However, not everyone is convinced. In education, particularly in the teaching of reading over the years, the choice of instructional methods has been heavily influenced by many factors, not only teachers' own frontline experiences about what works, but also politics, economics, and the popular wisdom of the day. The pendulum has swung back and forth between holistic, meaning-centered approaches and phonics approaches without much hope of resolving disagreements. Meanwhile, substantial scientific evidence has accumulated purporting to shed light on reading acquisition processes and effective instructional approaches.[6]

Our American way of organizing, funding, delivering, and evaluating education has fostered and tolerated such pendulum swings. The factors that contribute to these swings are present both at the universities where teachers receive their initial training and at local school districts, where decisions are made about how reading will be taught. Local schools are being pressured as never before to show positive results, but administrators are often not accountable for the viability of the programs and practices that they select.

Colleges of education are especially lacking in accountability for the quality of teacher preparation. Course content is still a matter of the instructor's individual preference—not governed by an accepted definition of what teachers need to know. There are relatively few checks and balances to ensure that university faculty teach the methods supported by scientifically conducted research or to ensure that future teachers are instructed in the specialized knowledge needed for teaching children to read, write, and spell. Teachers are more likely to be taught children's literature than cognitive psychology or linguistics. Teacher preparation courses rarely cultivate the habit of looking to credible research that would help future administrators and classroom teachers to select new reading materials for their district. Thus, when schools select instructional programs, they are seldom adopted on the basis of evidence that they work.

Teachers often express anger and dismay when they attend a workshop and learn what they should have been taught years earlier. A kindergarten teacher who has participated in professional development and coaching as part of a school-wide initiative to improve reading achievement told us, "I realize now that I really didn't know much about how to teach reading. I taught thematically, as I was instructed in my education classes. I never had kindergartners who read before this year. Now I am sad to think about all the children I could have helped prepare to read, if only I had known what to do."

Teachers want to do what is best for children, but if they have been given misinformation or have been misguided by administrators, they may not have the skills to teach reading by using the best practices. Because decision-making is more often driven by popular ideas than by evidence about what works best for most children, teachers also become very skeptical and prefer to learn from their own experience. In addition, they want a sense of control over what goes on in their classes, and they may have learned to trust their own intuition above all. Unfortunately, however, the core insights a teacher needs about teaching reading are often not discovered just from classroom experience. Thus, they do the best they can with the information and tools they have, and new fads continue to come along.

Is there a distinction between "research" and "scientific research"?

When we use the term "scientific research," we mean something specific. Scientific research meets the criteria established in the scientific community for the methods that will gradually lead to consensus about whether something is factually true or not. When researchers in a medical field evaluate new approaches to treating a medical condition, they rely on evidence obtained with research that meets acceptable standards. Some of the most important criteria for a study that is scientific are:

- A large enough sample of well-defined subjects so that the results can be generalized to other people.
- Objective researchers, with no affiliation to any company that might benefit from results of the research, and results that are reviewed by other objective people.
- Tests of competing hypotheses; the study should not set out to prove one hypothesis.
- Research that compares performance between groups that receive well-defined but different treatments.
- The inclusion of a control group that does not receive the experimental treatment or that receives a treatment that will probably not produce results.
- Quantitative measures of the outcome, so that causal statements can be made that a particular type of treatment leads to better results.

What are the most reliable sources of information about reading research?

As mentioned previously, the most recent summary of scientific research on reading is the report of the National Reading Panel called *Teaching Children to Read.* The subtitle of this report is significant: *An Evidence-Based Assessment of the Scientific Research Literature on Reading and Its Implications for Reading Instruction.* A thirty-page summary of the panel's findings, a four-hundred-page report of the panel's seven subcommittees, and a fifteen-minute video are available for free from the National Institute of Child Health and Human Development (NICHD). Another excellent publication that all kindergarten through third-grade teachers should have is called *Put Reading First*. This publication, distributed by the Department of Education, explains the NRP report in separate documents—one for teachers and another for parents. (See Appendix 2.)

The National Reading Panel report documents the work and conclusions of a committee that was commissioned by Congress in 1997. Congress asked the director of the NICHD, in consultation with the Department of Education, to convene a panel to "assess the status of research-based knowledge, including the effectiveness of various approaches to teaching children to read." The panel was composed of fourteen people, including leading scientists in reading research, representatives of colleges of education, reading teachers, educational administrators, child development experts, psychologists, and parents.

Other recent summaries of reading research include Marilyn Adams's book *Beginning to Read* (1990) and the National Research Council's *Preventing Reading Difficulties in Young Children* (1998). The National Reading Panel's work is distinguished because it began with a definition for scientifically acceptable research in reading.

After holding a series of regional hearings across the country to solicit public opinion, the panel developed seven broad topics to address. Initially, the panel conducted extensive searches of research databases to identify all research conducted on each of the seven topics. To determine which research studies would be included, the subcommittees assessed each study against the criteria for reliable research, such as sample size and diversity; whether the instructional interventions were so clearly defined that they could be replicated or copied by others; the quality of the study design; and the use of specific measures of results. A vast majority of existing research in reading could not be reviewed by the panel because the research did not meet scientific criteria. For example, in the work of the subcommittee studying phonics, only 38 of the 1,373 studies identified in the literature searches met the criteria and were included. Similarly, only 52 of 1,962 articles about phonemic awareness were included.

Reading education has long been plagued by low standards for research and overuse of the term "research-based." Perhaps this is why teachers have become wary of hearing that a product is based on research. In the case of the National Reading Panel, however, a rigorous standard was upheld. We speak to many audiences all over the country, however, and we seldom find educators who are familiar with this report.

What are the key conclusions of the National Reading Panel's work?

The panel reached the following major conclusions about effective reading instruction:

- *Explicit instruction in phonemic awareness (PA) improves a child's reading and spelling skills.* Phonemic awareness is the ability to focus on and manipulate the individual speech sounds in words. The panel recommends PA training in kindergarten and early first grade to provide children with an essential foundation in the alphabetic system. Although some children's brains are "wired" to learn this skill easily, many students need direct teaching. It is possible to develop PA through good teaching practices using enjoyable, gamelike activities in the classroom. The subgroup report of the panel stated that teaching children to manipulate the sounds in words not only helps them learn to read but also helps them spell better. Many research studies showed that with less than eighteen hours of explicit PA instruction, almost all children can reach a level of skill that will support reading, even children in low-performing schools who come from literacy-deficient homes.

• *Instruction in systematic phonics produces significant benefits for students in K to sixth grade and for children having difficulty in learning to read.* The ability to read and spell words was enhanced in kindergartners who received systematic beginning phonics instruction. First graders who were taught phonics systematically were better able to decode and spell, and they showed significant gains in their comprehension abilities. Across all grade levels systematic phonics instruction improves the spelling ability of good readers. The panel concluded that phonics instruction is not only useful but a necessary component of any good reading program.

• *In order to develop fluency in reading, it is more beneficial to have children read aloud with guidance and feedback, sometimes called guided oral reading, than to read silently without feedback.* There was not enough research support to validate whether the practice of sustained silent reading improves fluency.

• *It is important to teach children a variety of strategies to guide and improve reading comprehension.* Instructional strategies for which there was support included: learning how to monitor one's understanding of the material while reading; developing and answering questions about the text; learning to summarize the information; using the structure of the story to recall the events; and using graphic and semantic organizers (including story maps) to represent the material.

What is phonemic awareness, and why is it so important?

To be ready to read, a child not only needs to know the letters of the alphabet but also must be aware that her own speech is made up of segments that differ from letters. These segments are called phonemes. We try not to use educators' jargon in this book, but this term is worth learning because it is critical to understanding reading. Phonemic awareness is the ability to identify and manipulate the individual speech sounds in spoken words. Words can be divided into several other units such as syllables and rimes (rhyming parts), but the smallest unit of sound in our language is a phoneme. There are forty to forty-four phonemes in our language, depending on the classification system used. Phonemes do not correspond one-to-one with letters because some sounds are represented with two letters, such as *sh, ai, ow, th,* and *ng.* The awareness of the separate sounds in a word—phonemic awareness—is an auditory skill that underlies the ability to use an alphabet to read and write. A child who can recognize that the word *cat* has three speech sounds, the word *eye* has one, and the word *eat* has two possesses basic phonemic awareness. If a child can change the /m/ sound at the beginning of the word *man* to /r/ and know that the word is now *ran,* she has demonstrated an even greater degree of phonemic awareness.

She can compare the sounds in words, substitute a new sound for an old one, and blend the sounds to make a new word.

Success in learning phonics depends on basic phonemic awareness. Without a sense of the sounds that letters represent, the child approaches reading as rote memory of letter sequences. With phonemic awareness, the child can link letters to the sounds in words in order to decipher and spell them. Phonics is an approach to teaching reading in which the child is taught to associate letters with sounds and to use that knowledge to sound words out by blending the sounds from left to right.

You may also hear educators use the term "phonological awareness." This is a broader term than "phonemic awareness" and includes a number of other abilities. For example, the ability to distinguish rhyming words and syllable units and to divide sentences into words are phonological skills. These phonological skills are important, but the phonological skill most related to reading is phonemic awareness. Phonemic awareness is not the only skill you need, but you must have it in order to develop decoding and word recognition skill. It's like needing to know the finger positions for all the notes on a musical instrument before you learn to read music and play new pieces.

It has been known by scientists for at least fifteen years that phonemic awareness and letter knowledge are the two best predictors of how well a child will learn to read during her first two years of school. The National Reading Panel's report confirmed that instruction in PA helps children learn early reading skills. Here's what the panel said:

> Overall, the findings showed that teaching children to
> manipulate phonemes in words was highly effective

under a variety of teaching conditions with a variety of learners across a range of grade and age levels and that teaching phonemic awareness to children significantly improves their reading more than instruction that lacks any attention to PA.[7]

The panel emphasized that much more research is needed. There were not enough studies to comment extensively on the techniques that are most effective or the amount of instruction that is ideal. The panel did comment that, although PA training was effective regardless of its length, the ideal amount of time depends upon the student's needs and could be somewhere in the range of five to eighteen hours to be most effective.

Parents can help their child develop phonemic awareness through playlike activities. The resource list in Appendix 2 includes a list of books with activities for developing a child's phonemic awareness.

What did the National Reading Panel's report conclude about phonics instruction?

In examining the question of whether phonics instruction helps children learn to read more effectively than other types of instruction, the panel concluded:

> Findings provided solid support for the conclusion that systematic phonics instruction makes a bigger contribution to children's growth in reading than alternative programs providing unsystematic or no phonics instruction. . . . The conclusion drawn is that phonics instruc-

tion produces the biggest impact on growth in reading when it begins in kindergarten or first grade before children have learned to read independently.[8]

The panel defines "systematic phonics instruction" as follows:

Systematic phonics instruction typically involves explicitly teaching students a pre-specified set of letter-sound relations and having students read text that provides practice using these relations to decode words. Instruction lacking an emphasis on phonics instruction does not teach letter-sound relations systematically and selects text for children according to other principles. The latter form of instruction includes whole word programs, whole language programs, and some basal reader programs.[9]

Whole language teachers believe that phonics instruction should be integrated into meaningful reading or writing activities because children will discover naturally what they need to know about letter-sound correspondences. Many whole language teachers believe that teaching children the sound-letter correspondences in isolation and how to blend sounds will reduce a child's comprehension skills and turn children into "word callers." The panel directly addressed this concern:

Growth in reading comprehension is also boosted by systematic phonics instruction for younger students (below second grade) and reading disabled students.

These findings should dispel any belief that teaching phonics systematically to young children interferes with their ability to read and comprehend text. Quite the opposite is the case.[10]

Is it true that intervening early to solve a reading problem is more effective than later intervention?

Now that I am informed about reading difficulties, I feel that I have missed that crucial "window of opportunity," from ages five to six years old, for my daughter. I didn't get any support from her school, although I knew there was a problem as early as Christmas of her kindergarten year. Due to the public school's policy (they cannot classify a child as learning-disabled until she shows up two years behind where she should be), she was not tested until the end of first grade.

This parent, whose daughter is now in second grade, knew that her child was having learning difficulties early, yet the school's policies fostered delayed assessment and identification of children who needed intervention. Yes, intervention in kindergarten and first grade is more effective than intervention in fourth grade and beyond. Early intervention takes less time and fewer resources and serves to close the gap between good and poor readers much more effectively than remediation delivered later on. Many districts have begun using kindergarten screening tools to identify children at risk for reading difficulty starting in mid-kindergarten so that focused instruction can begin then, and children are watched carefully when they enter first grade. Every school district in the country should be instituting early screening and should be prepared to monitor children closely in first grade. Classroom teachers can screen students at minimal cost. Much is gained through preventive action, in both student achievement and students' self-esteem.

The state of Texas funded the development of the Texas Primary Reading Inventory in 1997 because then-governor Bush realized that children needed to be screened early. In the summers of 1999 and 2000, almost every kindergarten and first-grade teacher in Texas attended a summer Reading Academy to learn why some children fall behind, what kind of intervention is important, and how to carry it out. Second-grade teachers were instructed in the summer of 2001. This kind of focus on early intervention has been unusual, but it will most certainly reduce the number of children who fall behind.

In summary, early intervention is promoted by the National Institute of Child Health and Human Development because of these findings:[11]

- Eighty-five to 90 percent of *poor* readers can increase reading skills to average reading levels with prevention and early intervention programs that combine instruction in phonemic awareness, phonics, spelling, reading fluency, and reading comprehension provided by well-trained teachers.

- It takes four times as long to improve the skills of a struggling reader in fourth grade as it does to do so between mid-kindergarten and first grade. In other words, it takes two hours a day in fourth grade to have the same impact as thirty minutes a day in first grade.

• If intervention is not provided until nine years of age (the age that most children with reading difficulties first receive services at school), approximately 75 to 88 percent of these children will continue to have reading difficulties throughout high school and their adult lives.

Dr. Joseph Torgesen, one of the researchers who have contributed studies in support of these findings, expressed these ideas succinctly:

> The best solution to the problem of reading failure is to allocate resources for early identification and prevention. It is a tragedy of the first order that while we know clearly the costs of waiting too long, few school districts have in place a mechanism to identify and help children before failure takes hold. Indeed, in the majority of cases, there is no systematic identification until third grade, by which time successful remediation is more difficult and more costly. . . . to the extent that we allow children to fall seriously behind at any point during early elementary school, we are moving to a "remedial" rather than a "preventive" model of intervention. Once children fall behind in the growth of critical word reading skills, it may require very intensive interventions to bring them back up to adequate levels of reading accuracy, and reading fluency may be even more difficult to restore because of the large amount of reading practice that is lost by children each month and year they remain poor readers.[12]

In Chapter 5 we provide information about assessment tools for early screening of kindergarten through second-grade students. Some parents who learn about early screening after their child is older than six or seven worry about whether there is an age when it is too late for their child to catch up.

My daughter is seven and a half years old and in first grade (the oldest in her class) and is not reading or writing well. She has received extra help since September through the Title One program at school, but that doesn't seem to be helping much. She memorizes words and has a very difficult time remembering letter sounds and letter-combination sounds. Reading is a chore for her, and all the other kids seem to do it well in her class. Although I have suspected dyslexia since kindergarten, both her teacher this year and last year and her Title One teacher have downplayed that. I have requested testing. My question is, from everything I've read, the earlier the intervention takes place the better. Is seven and a half years old too late?

Although there *is* a crucial window of opportunity, you need to know that it is never too late. We teach older children to read all the time, although the instruction may be harder to arrange, it will take more time, and it will require an intense effort from the teacher and student. As Dr. Reid Lyon, chief of the NICHD, says, "While older children and adults can be taught to read, the time and expense of doing so is enormous compared to what is required to teach them when they are five or six years old."[13] The consequences of not learning to read well are so unacceptable that we almost never recommend giving up, no matter how much effort it takes.

At the end of kindergarten our son was still struggling with matching sounds to letters. His teacher recommended that we have him repeat kindergarten. We did, and it appeared to work. When he started first grade, he knew all his sounds and letters. He seemed ready to learn to read. Imagine our disappointment when he did not. At the end of first grade he still was not reading. We worked with him diligently over the summer, following all the advice we could gather. In second grade he began to receive extra support at school. In a sense it appeared that he could read. If we read a book to him, he could read it back to us word for word. But if we took a word out of the book—one he had read easily—and wrote it on a piece of paper, he had no idea what it was. What is more, he seemed to have no idea how to go about figuring out what it was. By the time he reached third grade he was basically a nonreader and began to experience real behavior problems. We tried everything we could think of. At one point, our son was seeing a child psychologist, an optometrist (who gave him exercises to improve his visual tracking), and a speech pathologist. But his behavior told us we were still not doing enough.

Just as it is heartbreaking for this parent to watch her child struggle, it is difficult for us to watch parents navigate their way alone through this maze. Unfortunately, this parent's story of wrong turns and confusing advice is all too common. This family is losing valuable time trying all these suggested steps, most of which sound ill informed. The extra help at school may not have been with an effective approach, or the intervention may not have been intense enough or long enough to help. The referral to the eye development specialist is most likely an uninformed recommendation, as few children have reading problems due to visual impairments. Some do, but the visual problems are not necessarily the cause of the reading difficulty, and the therapy prescribed may or may not relieve eyestrain or other focusing or scanning problems.

We advised this parent that the child needs good reading instruction in order to be able to detect the sounds in words, match them with letters, and sound them out in order to develop that "sight" vocabulary. The total program should include reading controlled word patterns in stories and writing those patterns. There is no such thing as a "sight word reader," who simply memorizes whole words.

Becoming informed is one of the greatest challenges parents face. When your child is having trouble learning to read, you will find yourself immersed in the problem. Suddenly, you are thrown into a whole new arena—one in which you may not feel very comfortable initially. But it is imperative that you get up to speed as quickly and efficiently as possible so that you can help your child. This book is your first step, but there are many other wonderful sources to learn more about specific topics. We have provided resource lists at the end of this book that we think will be helpful to parents.

chapter 3

Why You Are Your Child's Best Advocate

I think it is very important for parents to know what rights they have when it comes to their children and school issues. I was not informed of my child's rights. Our son had been on the honor roll for most of second and third grade, when his grades started to slip. We almost lost out on getting him the help he so desperately needed. We began asking why, but his teachers gave us answers like "He's not trying," "He's a lazy student," or "He's not applying himself." Unfortunately, because these were his teachers, we believed them, and our son continued to slip for the next two years. By sixth grade things were really bad. Not only was he looking at summer school, but possibly failing altogether. Finally, I had had enough. I knew something was not right. We got him tested and found out he is dyslexic. As most people with dyslexia are able to do, he was able to learn little tricks to use so no one would catch on that he was having problems. But finally, it caught up with him and got to be too much. I wish I had known I could have gotten the same type of testing through the school system—it would have saved us a lot of time. Now he is getting the help he needs, which includes work on phonics, and for the first time in four years is back on the honor roll and has been nominated for two different academic awards.

We have heard this story many times. Sensing that "something is not right," a parent continues to search until he or she gets answers that make sense. Time and again, the point at which a parent faces a child's learning problem is the turning point for the child's whole future.

Why didn't an educator notice that the boy's apparent apathy was a symptom, not a cause, of his declining grades? Educators, although they may be devoted to their work, may teach between twenty and a hundred children every day and cannot have the perspective that a parent has. In addition, there often are other students with more serious and dramatic needs that demand the attention of limited resources in the school. Students who are merely struggling academically may not draw attention to themselves until they act out, fail a course or two, or become perceptibly depressed.

Ultimately, the mother quoted above trusted her own intuition. Because she knew her son well, she was sure that her son's academic difficulties could not be explained by laziness. "Finally, I had had enough," she said. She knew that she had to get more involved, take a different approach, and seek outside help. Through networking, she found out how to have her child tested privately. With the diagnosis of specific reading disability (dyslexia) she was able to advocate for the special services that finally helped her son learn to read and cope with his assignments.

This story may raise several questions for parents:

- What is a parent's role when his or her child is struggling at school?

- What does it mean to be an advocate?
- Do I need to hire an attorney or professional advocate to get special services through the school?
- How can I learn to advocate for my child?

Does my child need an advocate?

For the many children who cope successfully with the school system, an advocate may never be necessary. However, for children who have difficulty in learning to read, an advocate is essential whether or not they have a learning disability.

What is an advocate? An advocate is someone who speaks on behalf of another person's needs and rights. A dictionary defines the word as "one who pleads the cause of another." An advocate does not need to be adversarial; in fact, being adversarial is generally not the most effective way to get what you want. An advocate is also someone who can say the right thing at the right time to get the job accomplished. One professional in the field likes to say, "Develop a language of persuasion rather than a language of positional battle."[1] If parents assume that the school system is looking out for their child, they may see no reason to get involved with a third party. Let's step back, however, and look at the way school systems are run and regulated to understand why your child may need an advocate who is not an employee of the school.

Schools are organizations. They have a management structure, rules and procedures, and unwritten modes of operating. Your child is assigned to a new teacher each year, and that teacher is responsible for teaching your child within the whole class. Communication between home and school is pro-

moted through regularly scheduled parent-teacher conferences, or conversations with the teacher in between conferences. If you are concerned about what is happening with
your child's education, you are encouraged to talk to your
child's teacher first. You may also choose to talk with the
principal, but typically any concerns you raise with the principal you will have first discussed with the teacher.

When your child has difficulty in learning to read, it
means one of several things: he has not or is not responding
to the kind of instruction available; he has a learning disability; or he experiences another kind of learning impairment,
either cognitive or emotional. Often the difficulty is com-
pounded by a combination of these circumstances.

If you suspect that your child is not learning to read with
the instruction that the teacher is providing, you may need to
seek a meeting with the principal. To circumvent the
teacher's authority and meet with the principal, however, may
create a different sort of problem for you later. First, the principal may not be any more knowledgeable about reading instruction and may not be of much help. Second, the classroom
teacher may share your concerns and may be making a referral to the child study team already. Third, if you want to gain
access to the school's resources, it is best to try to collaborate
with the classroom teacher. Thus, it is important to be forth-
right with the teacher about your concerns. The principal and
administration share responsibility for mobilizing the resources your child needs.

The principal typically has an annual budget for diagnostic testing and is usually part of the team that decides which
children will be tested. Moreover, you need to understand
that the principal is an administrator whose job is to manage

the needs of all the teachers and students, and to spend the school budget in a way that maximizes the education provided to all the students. Your child is just one of two hundred to five hundred children, depending on the size of your elementary school. Because of all these factors, your child can get lost in the system. It is also true that the "squeaky wheel" gets the most attention.

Your child needs an advocate because children in elementary school generally cannot speak for themselves. Your child can let you know that things are not right, but he doesn't know how to get what he needs within the school system. A six-year-old usually can't even tell you why he doesn't like school or if he is embarrassed that he can't read as well as his classmates. He may take a long time to get ready for school in the morning or he may bolt out of his classroom as fast as he can. All you know is that the joyful child you observe over the weekends is not the same child who walks out of the classroom at the end of a weekday. He often can't even tell you why. A child who is too young to speak up and get what he needs is obviously in need of an advocate. Even a child in junior high or high school needs an advocate when he is not effective at that role himself.

Can a school employee be your child's advocate?

A school employee cannot be the child's advocate. Although schools are concerned with the welfare and education of each child, they also must uphold the institution. The administrators must defend their employees, whose actions must comply with school policy and state laws. If the principal agrees with you and doesn't think that the teacher is providing instruction that is effective, she may not be free to tell you that, because she also has to respect the teacher's right to fair and confidential evaluation procedures. The principal would open the school to a potential lawsuit if she said that a teacher is not doing a good job, even if she believes that you are right. The principal's first concern is maintaining high morale and a sense of fair treatment among faculty so that the whole school operates well.

The principal must be concerned with the needs of all the students, not just the needs of one individual child. In making decisions about what services to offer, the principal has to take into account the school budget, the needs of all the children in the school (not just the children who need additional help), and the happiness of the faculty. She may listen and then later take a closer look herself at the instruction in the classroom, but it is unlikely that she will tell you her opinion.

Many teachers are dedicated to the welfare of each child in the class. Even those wonderful teachers, however, cannot act as your child's advocate. A teacher will only have your child for one year, and your child should have an adult advocate who takes a longer-term perspective. If your child's teacher goes too far out on a limb to support your child, she could be vulnerable to criticism from her principal, other parents, or other faculty. For example, if she agrees that an expensive service is needed, she may incur the wrath of those who feel that special services are draining the budget for the entire school. Parents should not be confused when a teacher privately encourages them to speak up and ask for particular services, yet seems quiet in a meeting when that very topic is discussed with the principal and other administrators. The teacher is not necessarily unsupportive, just aware of the system in which she works. You are the only person who remains the constant advocate for your child across all the years and all the different teachers your child will have in his lifetime.

Can I hire a professional advocate to help me?

Some parents hire a professional advocate to advise them on the process of obtaining special services for their child. An advocate is not usually an attorney, so obtaining advice from one is less expensive and less drastic than hiring a lawyer. Professional advocates often work in partnership with attorneys who specialize in the rights of students with disabilities. An advocate can also be any friend who supports you at meetings.

Parents turn to advocates either when they feel unable to navigate the special education process on their own or when they want someone at meetings who represents their interests exclusively. Meetings are often attended by many school personnel, and parents can easily feel outnumbered. An advocate may be a friend who can be a witness, take notes, and give support. Even though advocates are helpful because they know the system and can help you get the most from it, you are the irreplaceable, most qualified chief advocate.

You are the only person who knows the entire history of your child's pre-reading and reading education. When the school year begins, the teacher tries to assess the skills of each of the twenty to twenty-five new students in her class. Even if she realizes that your child seems to be "at risk" because of skills that are underdeveloped, she has no way of knowing whether his skills are weak because he hasn't had much prior instruction in that area or because he has a reading disability. Even if the child attended the same school for kindergarten, the first-grade teacher, for reasons of staff turnover, lack of meaningful documentation, or lack of time, may not have consulted the people who taught him earlier.

Why You Are Your Child's Best Advocate

- You are the only person who knows the history of your child's instruction.
- You know your child better than anyone else.
- You know your child's entire day and what other conflicts/stresses he is dealing with.
- You are the only person who has *only* your child's best interest in mind and are not balancing the needs of the classroom or school.
- You and your child, not the teacher, will live with the consequences of your child losing a year in learning to read.

You know what preparation your child had for reading. You know how much you and your child worked with magnetic letters on the refrigerator door, watched *Sesame Street*, sang the alphabet song, or played rhyming games. You know how many hours you read books aloud to your child. The hours you spent in word and letter play *do* make a difference. The teacher may assume for months that your child did not have as much preparation as other students and that he will catch up once she begins to teach him. You know differently.

My son's (Susan's) first-grade teacher kept reassuring me

that his problem was just a developmental lag and that he would catch up. She did not seem to realize that he was the oldest child in the class. We had held him back and had not started him in kindergarten at age five because his birthday was only a little more than a month from the cutoff date. In preschool we began to have concerns about him, most of which were actually social issues, so we reasoned that it would be best to give him an extra year to mature so he would be one of the oldest rather than one of the youngest children in his class. It turned out that some of what we saw were early warning signs of a reading disability, but we didn't know anything about that at the time.

I knew that my son's Montessori preschool experience included lots of exposure to the sounds in letters and that many of those activities had been multisensory and structured. His experiences included tracing letters in cornmeal, tracing sandpaper letters mounted on wood blocks, and exposure to easy, highly decodable books. This preschool experience clearly gave him some of the best preparation for reading. He should have found learning to read easy after this experience. But his teacher in first grade had no way of knowing how extensive his early preparation had been, and we never thought to tell her because we didn't know he was behind until after the midpoint of the year. His first-grade teacher either didn't realize his struggles or didn't share them with us until our son began expressing his frustration and we brought his problems to her attention. Many teachers don't want to alarm parents, so they hold off in providing this kind of feedback too early in the school year.

Not only does the teacher lack information about the student's previous instruction, but also the teacher's attention must be on twenty-five students and the management of the whole class. She has limited time to worry about any one student. It is impossible for a teacher to observe your child as closely as you do. You live with this child. You watch him try to do his homework, and you listen to him when he stumbles over words while reading to you. The teacher hears your child read a word or sentence at a time probably daily, but is lucky if she can listen to him read one-on-one uninterrupted for fifteen minutes each week. You may be listening to your child read fifteen minutes each day. The kinds of things you know about your child's reading include:

- What level of books he can read without much difficulty.
- How often he stumbles on words while reading a given text.
- Which words he can recognize almost instantly.
- Whether he can sound out unknown words.
- The degree to which he relies on pictures, initial consonant sounds, or context clues to figure out unknown words.

Never underestimate how important your perspective on your child's experiences is in comparison to the perspective of professionals. Here is a parent's description of her daughter as an example of how much a parent knows about her child's reading:

I have an adopted daughter who is nearly seven years old whom I am worried about. She recognizes only about fifteen out of twenty-six letters of the alphabet. She does not know *sounds* at all!!! I have taken her for hearing tests and they tell me there is nothing wrong with her hearing. Every time we suggest to her that she look at a word and figure out the sound, she panics and says, "You do it!" I've been told she is a tactile learner. I tried making letters out of things like macaroni and rice, but when she feels she's in a spot where she should say and know the letter, she freezes. I took her to a tutor and the woman says she's not ready to learn to read. I have been reading to her from the day I brought her home from the orphanage and she loves books. I asked if she should be evaluated at school. The study team found nothing wrong and her teacher feels quite confident that she is OK. They said, "Wait for first grade. Then if there is a problem we will know for sure." I just don't feel I can sit back and wait because I'm convinced that something is wrong.

The child is demonstrating plenty of warning signs that either she is dyslexic or she has not been taught phonics well enough to be able to sound out unknown words fluently. Any time a child is having trouble recognizing letters and associating sounds with letters at nearly seven years of age, you need to find out why.

The professionals at school may have only a superficial or partial understanding of your child. The psychologist may have tested him, yet she spent only a very small amount of time with him, and that time was spent in an atypical setting. Teachers may miss or misinterpret a child's behavior because they see it from only one perspective. In order to ensure that observations about a child are comprehensive and representative, special education laws mandate that a whole team of people who know the child be involved in determining eligibility for special education services. The special education law is explicit about all the school personnel who must be present at meetings.

Another reason why you are the best advocate is that your child may be able to talk to you more openly about what is upsetting him than he can talk to anyone at school. Home and family life provides a safe haven for many children with reading difficulties. The parent is the person in a child's life who understands him better than anyone else, and who listens to him with empathy. He may be reluctant to express his feelings of frustration about his reading with his teacher. Think of yourself as the translator. You listen to him talk, process what he says, and put his feelings into words that make the message meaningful to the teacher and principal. If your child is complaining about not wanting to go to school, then you need to find out why. He might tell you how he felt when he had to read aloud to the class and he stumbled over many words. He might tell you about how he felt when everyone was staring at him, or when Johnny called him "stupid" on the playground because he can't read. He probably won't use the word "embarrassed," but you can articulate that feeling when you tell his teacher what is bothering him about school.

How can I learn to advocate for my child?

Learning to advocate is just like learning anything else. It is learned in steps. First, you accept your role. Next, you begin to read. Then you seek advice and other resources. Soon you are devising a strategy, setting goals, and following through.

Tips on Being an Effective Advocate
for Your Child

- *Become informed.* Know your family's legal rights and responsibilities, procedural rights, how to measure progress, how to create a paper trail of all conversations and meetings, and how to write strong, measurable IEP (individualized education plan) goals. Start by requesting a copy of your rights from your local school district.

- *Learn how to advocate for your child.* Read books and articles, attend conferences and workshops, and network with other parents. Inquire about services offered by your state parent training and information centers, which are organizations that receive federal funding from the Individuals with Disabilities Education Act to provide help to parents. Know when to hire an advocate or attorney.

- *Get organized.* Periodically request copies of your child's records and keep them in a notebook organized chronologically.

- *Document everything.* The best way to avoid litigation is to assume that it will happen and prepare for it from the beginning. Keep a log or journal with notes about every phone call, write letters to document all meetings and conversations, have private evaluations done periodically, and tape-record meetings and then transcribe the tape.

- *Get independent second opinions.* Hire outside experts to give you an independent opinion on whether your child is on grade level, and what level of progress has been made.

cont.

- *Don't assume that the school will advocate for your child* with his best interests in mind; there are other interests that the school must protect as well.
- *Develop your own political power within the school system.* Network with other parents and join any groups of parents that will help you.
- *Be pleasant but firm.*

Your quest to be informed must include not only the research on effective reading instructional practices but also information about how the educational system works. Another important responsibility is judging whether an educational program is likely to be helpful.

I have a son who is in second grade and will be nine in August (we held him back in preschool). I believe he has dyslexia, although repeated testing has failed to give us this diagnosis. He is the oldest in his class and one of the poorest readers. He has been going to a Wilson-trained tutor since the beginning of first grade, and his tutor has just recommended a computer program that requires a huge time commitment. He is a pretty active boy and I think that four hours a day for four to six weeks would be really difficult.

This mother is skeptical about the time the child would spend on the computer, and whether, given his high activity level, he would benefit from such a program. She might ask for a trial session to evaluate the effect of the four-hour session on her child before she commits to the entire program. She might also ask to see independent evidence that the program is, indeed, effective for students like her son. Fast ForWord (see Chapter 7), for example, has not been independently shown to treat reading problems in school-aged children.

Another family faced a similar question:

> My six-year-old son has been identified as having a central auditory processing disorder. I've had a consultation with a trained Lindamood-Bell professional. It seems that his comprehension problems are far worse than his phonological problems. This came as quite a shock, but once things were explained to me, his patterns of confused behavior through the years now make complete sense. To deal with this, I have scheduled approximately twenty hours of treatment at a clinic. However, this center is so far away from home, I'm afraid that my son's quality of life will suffer if we're constantly on the road (about three hours one way), and he will become rebellious toward the entire process. As things now stand, he has a good attitude toward things. I don't want to risk losing that.

The long drive through rural Kentucky to the Lindamood-Bell clinic (described in Chapter 7) sounds daunting. Sometimes, however, we do not know the effect of a program on us or our children until we give it a try. The summer after my (Susan's) son finished fifth grade he rode in the car for two hours a day to receive four hours of tutoring every day for five weeks. I, too, worried that the long drive would cause him to dread the tutoring. To my surprise, he did not resist it. He used the time to listen to favorite CDs and read in the back-seat of the car. By this time, spelling and writing were more problematic than reading. Under what other circumstance would he have read for two hours a day that summer? But for families who feel stranded in rural areas, more and more on-line alternatives are becoming available, such as the home tutoring service at the Greenwood Institute in Putney, Vermont, or the K12.com curriculum designed for home instruction. Seek alternative solutions and try them out.

What legal rights does my child have to testing and special services?

All children have a legal right to a free and appropriate education in the United States. The Individuals with Disabilities Education Act (IDEA) specifies that school systems must provide students with disabilities, including students with learning disabilities, an education that meets their unique needs. This act, initially passed in 1975, was updated in 1997. The update specifies even more clearly the role of parents as equal participants in the decisions related to a child's education.

You must know these rights to obtain effective and appropriate instructional services for your child. School systems may not be following the complex rules of special education procedures because they are burdensome and time-consuming. If parents learn about their rights and discover major procedural violations, they may be able to achieve an agreement with the school about a program more easily. It appears to be rare that parents sue a school system just because procedures were not followed, but there are safeguards in place for your protection. Before you are able to recognize any procedural violations, however, you need to know what they are. Here is one parent's perspective:

I am struggling every day with the problems of my son. He is now eleven years old, in the fifth grade, and is severely dyslexic. We have found no answers or programs that seem to help. His school has written him off, and is not willing to try any new ideas. As a matter of fact, I will be going to his parent-teacher conference today—a week after all the other conferences have ended. Most everything they now do with him is the total opposite of what I have read in books and on websites about how to teach a dyslexic student. He too is discouraged and upset. He cries daily over his reading, to the point where he has begged me to help him. Only I am lost. I am looking for a new program to help him, although I don't know enough about the different types of reading programs to research them. I too am dyslexic, although not as severely as my son.

We advise this parent to attend a workshop on her legal rights under special education law, and to do a lot of reading. Free workshops are offered for parents to learn about their legal rights; you can locate the agency that provides these workshops in your state through the National Information Center for Children and Youth with Disabilities, which is listed in Appendix 2 of this book. We have devoted an entire chapter of this book to providing an overview of the IEP process, along with a list of recommended resources in Appendix 2.

In summary, you know your child better than anyone else—including his teacher. You are the *only* person who is focused exclusively on your child's best interests. You know you cannot afford advice or opinions that are misinformed or that will lose valuable time. You must challenge what you suspect is not working well. You and your child will live with his academic successes and failures throughout his life. In order to advocate well, parents need to know what to ask for, what their legal rights are, and how to apply pressure to get what they know their child needs. It is primarily up to you to obtain educational and psychological support for your child.

chapter 4

Identifying the Problem

> When our son was in kindergarten and we suspected dyslexia, we were told that he would "grow out of his reversal problems," and it was too early to detect anything long-term. That was four years ago. I have assumed that we were given very poor information. Have advances been made to test young children?

There are ways to detect potential reading difficulties even before first grade. Early screening is so important we have provided a list of early assessment tools in Appendix 1. All of them measure the critical pre-reading and language skills most useful for determining how easily a child will learn to read.

Children struggle to learn to read for several reasons, including insufficient preschool preparation, insufficient instruction once they are in school, and innate difficulty with the specific language processing skills that underlie reading. Not all children who show early warning signs will be dyslexic, but dyslexia can be identified early with considerable accuracy. We will use the term "reading difficulty" to refer to any undefined delay in learning to read, and the term "dyslexia" for a problem in the child's constitutional makeup that will cause a series of challenges with school. Dyslexia is a language-based learning disability (discussed later in Chapter 4 in detail). Reading difficulty may be evident when a child is five years of age, and it is important to know what to look for. Let's first consider some statistics on reading skill.

How many people are affected by reading difficulties?

Reading difficulty is so common in our society that the National Institutes of Health (NIH) have referred to it as a major public health problem. We have a higher illiteracy rate than Sweden, Finland, and Cuba, among other countries. About 25 percent of adults in our society are functionally illiterate, according to the United States Department of Labor Statistics, whereas in Sweden the estimate of illiteracy is between 3 and 7 percent. Illiteracy is even more common among individuals who are incarcerated, single teenage mothers, and persons dependent on public assistance. For the past fifteen years, Congress has appropriated steadily increasing amounts of money to the NIH to study who has difficulty in learning to read, what causes that difficulty, and the long-term impact of reading poorly. Although appropriations increased after 1987, the NICHD (National Institute of Child Health and Human Development), the branch of the NIH that has studied reading development and reading difficulties, began funding research in reading in 1965. Dozens of research sites across the United States and Canada have studied more than 35,000 participants, two-thirds of whom are skilled readers and one-third of whom are impaired readers.

Summaries of the NICHD's studies of reading estimate

that 17 to 20 percent of children nationwide are likely to experience serious problems with reading unless they receive intensive, well-designed instruction. In addition, children in the "slow reader" range—those who simply don't read very well, who don't enjoy reading, and who don't read of their own accord—constitute an estimated additional 20 percent. These data emerge from several long-term research projects, including the Connecticut Longitudinal Study conducted by the Yale Center for Learning.

Researchers at the Yale Center randomly selected and tracked the reading development of more than 350 kindergarten children in Connecticut from the age of five through early adulthood. The longitudinal design of the work—wherein hundreds of children are followed for a good portion of their lives—is unusual. It gives a more complete picture than research conducted on children who have already failed to learn.

When the entire sample of children was studied across many classrooms and schools in Connecticut, several key findings emerged. First, the number of children struggling with reading was far greater than the 5 to 6 percent typically served in the special education system.[1] Second, reading disabilities affected girls at roughly the same rate as boys, although boys were four times more likely to be referred for assessment and extra help. Boys, it seems, were more likely to misbehave and have coexisting problems maintaining their attention and getting work done in the classroom.[2] Finally, the problems children experienced were evident as early as kindergarten and were not outgrown by any more than one-fourth of the students.

Research Insights

- Reading problems affect 17 to 20 percent of children.
- They affect girls as often as boys.
- Children are unlikely to just grow out of them.

Is it likely that my first grader is simply experiencing a developmental lag?

Although children do develop at different rates, attributing reading failure to immaturity is risky and usually unhelpful. Children who are poor readers at the end of first grade most often are poor readers in fourth grade. The evidence comes from the following reports:

Research Studies about Poor Readers
Not Catching Up

- 74 percent of children who were poor readers in third grade remained poor readers in ninth grade (Francis 1996).[3]
- 9 of 10 children deficient in reading in first grade were poor readers in fourth grade (Juel 1988).[4]
- 8 of 10 children with severe word reading problems at the end of first grade were below average at the beginning of third grade (Torgesen 1997).[5]

Early signs of reading difficulty should not be ignored or passed off to immaturity. Maturity and readiness are concepts that have some value, but they do not explain specific behavior such as confusing letters, forgetting letter names, or associating the wrong sound with a letter. Social maturity at age five or six is not directly related to the ability to hear sounds in words, associate letter sounds with letter names, or know how a book is read. There is little to support a "wait and see if she grows out of it" position. The safest assumption is that early, direct teaching designed to help the child through the first steps of learning to read will minimize risks later on.

As we stated earlier, the time you spend waiting for a child to "catch up" is the best window of opportunity for teaching her deliberately what she needs to know. If we teach the sounds, letters, words, and language comprehension skills that will lead to good reading by the end of first grade, most children will avoid failure. There is no known advantage to waiting. At the very worst, help might be given to a child who is among those few who would have eventually learned to read well without help. On the whole, delayed intervention is costlier to everyone, including the child. She is more likely to develop confidence, enjoy reading, read more, and read better if she gets off to a good start.

Parents still cannot count on well-informed early intervention practices in every classroom. Your own state Department of Education and your local school board may need to be introduced to critical research findings to join the numerous districts that are trying to prevent reading failure. If you are looking for information about early intervention, we recommend Joseph Torgesen's "Catch Them Before They Fall," *American Educator,* 1998 (see Appendix 2 for how to obtain a copy of this article).

Reasons Not to Wait to Intervene

- The longer you wait, the more hours of intervention will be needed in the end.
- Waiting increases the chance that your child will never catch up.
- There is a greater risk of loss of self-esteem as your child fails for a longer period.
- The child misses out on the reading content and vocabulary growth that her peers are getting.
- The longer she struggles in learning to read, the higher the probability that she will never love reading.

How early can a child be identified as at risk for reading failure?

If schools follow research recommendations, they will screen children no later than mid-kindergarten and evaluate those at risk before they enter first grade. Children's skills can be assessed in several key areas: phonemic awareness, letter knowledge, sound-letter association, language comprehension, and familiarity with the way books are read. The best early screening tools are 80 to 90 percent accurate in sorting children into those at risk and those who are likely to do well in reading.

Screening tools are more reliable when they are given in mid-kindergarten than at the beginning of kindergarten because many children come to school not knowing how to focus their attention or comply with expectations of the classroom.[6] Accuracy in screening is even greater at the beginning of first grade, but the goal of an early identification and intervention program is to stimulate pre-reading skills in those children whose skills are weak so that they can be better prepared for first grade. Screening by a trained educator takes a few minutes for each child. More in-depth testing of children who fail a screen takes an additional fifteen minutes. The cost of a screening tool such as the Texas Primary Reading Inventory (TPRI) is minimal, about three dollars per child for a class of twenty. The National Reading Panel report recommended that every school institute a program of kindergarten and early-first-grade screening using a well-validated instrument.

What assessment tools can a school use to identify children with reading difficulties early?

There are a number of screening and assessment tools available now, and more are being developed even as we write. Several are available through education textbook publishers and others through state education agencies. One of the best has been developed and distributed by the Texas Education Agency—the Texas Primary Reading Inventory. Standardized testing in Texas begins in grade 3, but then-governor Bush and the Texas legislature realized that K–2 teachers needed a way to find and teach children at risk before they failed. The Texas Education Agency contracted with a research center in Houston to develop an instrument that teachers could use in grades K, 1, and 2.

The TPRI is sold as a kit ($78 for schools outside of

Texas). Teachers should have a daylong workshop to learn the techniques of administration, scoring, and interpretation. This kit also includes an Intervention Guide with instructions for activities and games to enhance a student's skills if they are weak on the assessment.

Virginia has also developed, tested, and validated an early screening instrument, called PALS. The State Department of Education collects data from all participating classrooms so that the instrument can be refined and the characteristics of children can be measured on a wide scale. A team of experts is also developing an on-line service for teachers to help them learn what to do when children appear to be at risk for difficulty. The PALS website is listed in Appendix 1.

One of the best commercially available early screening instruments is Fox in a Box, designed by Marilyn Adams for McGraw-Hill. A simple, brief literacy readiness screening tool for four- and five-year-olds has also been developed by Grover Whitehurst for the National Center for Learning Disabilities (NCLD). It is available over the Internet and is intended for wide use by parents and caretakers in day-care centers. See Appendix 1 for both of these assessment tools.

What kind of skills are assessed in these kindergarten and first-grade reading assessment tools?

Even ten years ago, readiness tests contained general indicators of maturity, intelligence, and motor skills, but did not assess the specific skills that most reliably tell us whether a child is likely to respond well to reading instruction. We used to think that we could learn about reading readiness by having children draw pictures, copy shapes, answer questions about the world in general, manipulate objects, and tell a story. We now know that those skills are not as effective at predicting good or poor reading as those involving awareness of speech sounds, letters, and reading itself. The following exercises are examples of the kind of tasks assessed by the most valid and useful screening instruments:

Example of Tasks
Included on Kindergarten Assessment

Letter name	Student is shown a letter and asked to name it.
Letter sound	Student is shown a letter and asked to name the sound(s) that it represents.
Blending onset-rime	Examiner says "f" followed by "ill," and student is asked what word these two word parts make when combined.
Print awareness	Student is asked to show examiner where to start reading a book, to frame where a sentence starts and ends, to point to a capital letter, etc.
Rhyming	Examiner says three words and asks the child which one doesn't rhyme (house, mouse, hat).

cont.

Blending phonemes	Examiner says the sound of the word *map* — /m/, /a/, /p/—and student says "map."*
Detecting initial sounds	Examiner instructs the student to "Say 'cup.' Now say 'cup' without the /k/" *(up)*.
Detecting final sounds	Examiner instructs the student to "Say 'beam.' Now say 'beam' without the /m/" *(bee)*.
Detecting middle sound	Examiner instructs the student to "Say 'sling.' Now say 'sling' without the /l/" *(sing)*.
Letter to sound linking	Examiner lays out three letters *(p, w, d)* and asks the student to identify which letter is at the beginning of *dog*.
Listening comprehension	After examiner reads a passage to the child, several comprehension questions are asked.

*A letter surrounded by slash marks (i.e., /m/) indicates that the reader is to pronounce the sound associated with the letter, not the letter name.

If your child can do these tasks easily at the middle of her kindergarten year, then her pre-reading skills are probably on track. If not, then you may want to find an experienced teacher who can give her one of the better screening tools available.

If your school doesn't do this kind of assessment and won't

do it with your encouragement, then you will want to consider having your child assessed privately. (See Chapter 5 for advice on how to find someone to assess your child.)

What characteristics will I observe if my child has a reading difficulty?

Children who are at risk for reading failure usually have the phonological processing problems described in Chapter 2. They experience unusual problems in detecting the speech sounds in spoken words, pronouncing new words and remembering them, breaking words apart into sounds, and blending sounds together into words. In addition, they have related problems in remembering the names and sounds of the letters. When they come to new words, they prefer to guess at them because they are not good at figuring out the sounds or blending them together.

Children with these problems often have unusual or noticeable problems in expressing themselves verbally. Their retelling of a movie plot may be either sparse or garbled. They may not comprehend questions, and they get all tangled up in long sentences. On the other hand, their problems may be very specific to print, and there may be no obvious related oral, or spoken, language problems.

You may see some signs of difficulty during the kindergarten year if your child is exposed to phonemic awareness activities at school or at home and has trouble doing these kinds of tasks. Pay attention if your child dislikes rhymes, matching sounds, changing sounds, or playing with new words. By the end of kindergarten, children should be writing words that contain at least most of the consonant sounds in a word, even though the vowels will often be missing or inaccurate. The following examples of children's writing samples will help you know how to look for evidence of skills that are developing on time and those that are delayed.

Typical Children's Writing, by Stage

Stage of Development	Typical Spellings
Pre-alphabetic	Dirrdckecat: "I love my teacher."
Early phonetic (late kindergarten)	YECIEBWOMNF: "Why should I be warm enough?"
Later phonetic (early to mid-grade 1)	ILAKTOETPESAACOILTOGRAKPAP: "I like to eat pizza. Also I like to drink pop."
Early conventional (late grade 1)	We did not plat ane seds it was prity and nas to see and lits of bamblbs came to git hany: "We did not plant any seeds; it was pretty and nice to see and lots of bumblebees came to get honey."

Many parents do not see the signs of a developing problem until mid-first grade when their child begins to struggle with reading itself. Ask your child's teacher lots of questions during the fall parent-teacher conference. Often parents are uncertain about what to ask their child's teacher, so we have provided a list.

Sample Questions to Ask Kindergarten Teacher

Questions to ask your child's teacher in the middle of kindergarten

1. Does my child show an interest and actively participate in activities related to reading?
2. Have you assessed my child's pre-reading skills? Have you assessed her phonemic awareness skills through a screening instrument such as the TOPA (Test of Phonological Awareness) or the TPRI (Texas Primary Reading Inventory)? If you haven't, would you consider doing it if I bring you the information about the assessment kit?
3. How many of the twenty-six letters of the alphabet does my child know?
4. How many of the forty-four phonemes does my child know?
5. When you analyze my child's invented spelling, what observations do you make about her knowledge of phonemes?
6. What activities are you doing in the classroom that explicitly develop phonemic awareness skills? How does my child perform on these activities?

Sample Questions to Ask First-Grade Teacher

Questions to ask your child's teacher in the fall of first grade

1. How is my child's progress in reading?
2. Have you assigned her to a specific reading group?
3. How many of the forty-four phonemes does my child know?
4. What type of approach to reading instruction are you teaching?
5. Are you teaching the letter-sound associations directly? If so, can you show me the sequential order of instruction?
6. Do you use decodable books at the beginning of the year?
7. Are you familiar with the report of the National Reading Panel?
8. How many common sight words does my child recognize?
9. When will you start requiring proper spelling of particular words previously studied?
10. Can you show me some samples of my child's writing and show me how closely her invented spelling is to the sounds in words?
11. What kind of assessments do you give to evaluate reading progress? Any measures of phonemic awareness such as the TOPA (Test of Phonological Awareness) or the TPRI (Texas Primary Reading Inventory)?
12. What can I do to help my child's reading development?

Be sure to ask your child to read to you once she has some skills under her belt. Your child may want you to do all the reading, but it is important to obtain a book at the right beginner level and listen to what she can do. During the first semester of first grade your child should be able to read simple books with mostly consonant-vowel-consonant words. She should recognize by sight some words such as *the, and, is,* and *was.* These are words to which she has been exposed so often that she should know them instantly. She will have seen them on the big books placed on the easel at school, on the word wall in the classroom, on flash cards her teacher sent home, or in books she has already read. As she reads to you, observe what she does when she tries to figure out a word she doesn't know by sight. When she reaches an unknown word, does she sound it out, or does she guess from a picture, the context, or an initial consonant sound? If your child has trouble decoding the sounds, you need to know that she is being taught the sounds before you assume that she cannot remember or apply them.

Possible Signs of a Reading Difficulty

- Resists reading aloud to you, although loves to listen to you read.
- Reading seems like a laborious task to her.
- Complains that reading is hard.
- Is in the lowest reading group, or is behind her peers.
- Feels embarrassed about reading aloud at school or around peers.
- Has difficulty in sounding out unknown words.
- Has difficulty with common words seen many times before.
- Relies on memorizing words rather than figuring them out.
- Guesses rather than sounds out an unknown word.

If reading is a laborious task that your child does not enjoy, you need to know why. Some children complain that reading is too hard and others suffer in silence, but you need to determine the nature and severity of the difficulty.

What is a learning disability?

The definition of "learning disability" (LD) varies according to the source. A legal definition is part of the Individuals with Disabilities Education Act (IDEA). Other definitions have been developed by various agencies and organizations. In addition, each state has its own way of determining who may receive special education services in that category. Thus, you may be learning-disabled in one state but not in another.

A learning disability is an unexpected and unusual difficulty in learning a specific skill. The term was coined in about 1968, when the federal government first included children with learning disabilities under protective legislation. There are many types of learning disabilities; dyslexia is one of these.

Most individuals with a learning disability experience difficulty in ways that stand out in relation to their other abilities, and in relation to what nondisabled children experience. For example, a child with a reading disability may learn math as effortlessly as her peers. Dr. Sally Shaywitz, one of the nation's leading researchers in this field, describes LD as "a weakness in a sea of strengths." The ability to decode print is not closely correlated with other aspects of intelligence, so an individual child may have talents and abilities in other areas. Some are good at mechanical, artistic, and spatial tasks; others are verbally precocious, have extensive oral vocabularies, and have analytical skills that are very strong. Some are natural leaders and are socially perceptive. Others may not be out of the ordinary in any way except for their inability to learn certain kinds of information as easily as others do. The person with a learning disability can learn, but may learn more slowly and only with the help of expert instruction by a well-trained teacher or tutor. Typically, the child has to expend more effort than other children to master that domain of learning.

There are many types of learning disabilities and many different terms used to describe them. Here are some of the common terms to describe and classify learning disabilities:

- *Dyslexia*—a language-based learning disability in which a person has trouble decoding print, reading with fluency, spelling, and writing.
- *Dysgraphia*—a writing disability in which a person finds it hard to form letters, produce sustained and legible handwriting, and translate language into the handwritten form.
- *Dyscalculia*—a mathematical disability in which a person has a difficult time calculating accurately and quickly, solving arithmetic problems, or grasping math concepts.
- *Nonverbal learning disability* (NLD). This term is not well defined from a scientific perspective, but is used for a number of learning disorders that are not language-based. They include problems with spatial judgment and orientation, understanding how the parts of something fit into a whole, and understanding mathematical and scientific logic. The term is also used for social and communication problems in which a person cannot "read" facial expressions, gestures, body posture, and conversational cues.

In addition to these terms for different types of learning disabilities, you may also hear quasi-medical terms such as "developmental learning disorder," "neuropsychological dysfunction," "auditory processing disorder," "visual processing disorder," or "specific language disability." Different terms are often used for the same set of symptoms. There is also a variety of terms that relate to attention and self-regulated behavior, such as "attention deficit disorder" (ADD), "attention deficit hyperactivity disorder" (ADHD), and "executive functioning difficulties"; disorders of attention are classified separately from learning disabilities. Individuals may be affected by only one type of learning disability or may have more than one. Difficulty in learning to read (dyslexia) is the most common type of learning disability, affecting more than 80 percent of people with learning disabilities.[7] Between 30 and 50 percent of those who are dyslexic also meet the criteria for having attention deficit hyperactivity disorder.

There has always been disagreement among people in the field of learning disabilities about the benefits and drawbacks of "labeling." Some advocates have argued that labeling children can negatively affect their self-esteem and that classification does not provide useful information about the child's unique needs and strengths. They prefer to use terms that they believe are less negative, such as "learning difference," "learning style issue," or "learning difficulty" instead of "learning disability." For this book we have chosen to use the term "learning disability" because within our current educational system there are laws that employ this term to ensure the rights of children to an appropriate education. We may use less definitive terms such as "learning difficulty" in referring to common problems that would not be severe enough to qualify a child for special services. Until our schools achieve the ideal state of serving every child's educational needs without diagnoses or labels, we support using terms that are helpful in obtaining access to resources.

Before leaving the topic of definitions and labels, it is important to mention that many of the organizations that serve people with learning disabilities recommend using what is called "person-first language." These organizations advocate that rather than saying "a learning-disabled individual," it is preferable to say "an individual with a learning disability," making the disability a single characteristic and not an all-encompassing label.

What is dyslexia?

"Dyslexia" is a commonly misunderstood term. If we surveyed people on the street to see what they know about dyslexia, a large majority would associate it with the reversal of letters such as *b* and *d,* with mirror writing, or with "seeing things backward." Although some individuals with dyslexia do reverse letters or confuse letters that are similar, this trait is *not* the defining characteristic of dyslexia. The International Dyslexia Association has produced two definitions of dyslexia, one formulated by the research community and one formulated by practitioners who provide remedial services to individuals with the condition.

According to the research community:
Dyslexia is one of several distinct learning disabilities. It is a specific language-based disorder of constitutional origin characterized by difficulties in single word decod-

ing, usually reflecting insufficient phonological processing abilities. These difficulties in single word decoding
are often unexpected in relation to age and other cognitive and academic abilities; they are not the result of generalized developmental disability or sensory impairment.
Dyslexia is manifested by variable difficulty with different forms of language, often including, in addition to
problems reading, a conspicuous problem with acquiring
proficiency in writing and spelling.[8]

According to practitioners:

Dyslexia is difficulty with language. For people with
dyslexia, intelligence is not the problem. The problem is
language. They may have difficulty with reading,
spelling, understanding language they hear, or expressing
themselves clearly in speaking or in writing. An unexpected gap exists between their potential for learning and
their school achievement.[9]

In Chapter 2 we discussed the importance of *phonemic
awareness* as a necessary condition to being able to learn to
read. The weakness in basic language skill common in dyslexia is not caused by either a vision or a hearing problem.
The person's eyes and ears function normally in most cases;
rather, the problem resides with the brain's interpretation of,
and memory for, the information that reaches it through the
eyes and ears. Individuals with dyslexia have trouble recognizing, blending, separating, and remembering the speech
sounds (phonemes) that letters represent. As a consequence,
they have trouble learning to associate the letter patterns in
print with their sounds.

If word recognition is not fast and accurate, comprehension will suffer. Comprehension depends on being able to translate the print back into speech *automatically*—that is, without conscious effort or attention. Individuals with dyslexia can learn to read, but are likely to need very explicit and systematic training that includes building speed and automaticity. Most teachers swear by multisensory learning techniques to engage children's attention and help them remember.[10]

People with dyslexia *can* be taught to read successfully; however, the individual must have an unwavering determination to persevere in learning something that is inherently very difficult. Parents and educators play a critical role in supporting and helping to motivate the person with dyslexia. Often the person survives school with the support of mentors and family members and involvement in some activity that provides self-esteem.

Dyslexia is unrelated to socioeconomic status or the parent's level of education. It occurs across all socioeconomic groups, although children from poorly educated families are more likely to experience serious problems because they have often not been talked to, read to, or led to books the way more advantaged children have been. Poor children with dyslexia are also more likely to attend schools that do not provide the expert instruction needed to help them along.

Children with dyslexia may be very bright, average, or below average in intellectual ability. IQ is not closely related to the ability to read in the beginning stages of learning because phonological processing is fairly independent of IQ. The child who is both highly gifted and dyslexic may experience extreme internal conflict between ease of learning in some subjects and learning difficulty in reading and spelling. The child might feel like a composite of pieces that just don't fit together. This feeling of being "unglued" is disconcerting and can lead to depression if not identified.

Dyslexia runs in families. Geneticists report that there is a predisposition to dyslexia that is inherited or passed down from generation to generation. The predisposition or vulnerability to developing the symptoms is best measured on phonological tasks, such as the ability to rhyme, spell or say nonsense words, or talk in pig Latin. On these tasks, family members tend to perform similarly. Researchers have even identified genes and chromosomes that probably carry this trait.

Given the fact that children are more or less hardwired for processing language at the speech sound level, children who have had excellent literacy and oral language environments at home may still have trouble learning to read. The amount parents read aloud to their children will not be the primary determining factor in how easily their child learns to read. Parents who have spent hours and hours reading to their children and playing with letters and letter sounds are likely to be shocked when they see that their child struggles to learn to read. Reading aloud, using good conversational skills, and encouraging language expression are all extremely important, but they will not inoculate children against dyslexia.

Two different kinds of research have led to new insights about how the brain of a person with dyslexia processes information. One type of research has involved taking images of a person's brain while reading; the other type has examined the brains of dyslexic individuals donated to laboratories upon the individuals' death. The imaging research uses functional magnetic resonance imaging (fMRI) to study the areas of the brain that are activated as the person attempts language and reading tasks. By comparing images of people with and without dyslexia, researchers have confirmed important functional differences. The person with dyslexia activates frontal areas of the left hemisphere and typically has less activation in the posterior language areas.

A recent paper explains it this way:

> New, objective ways to assess putative brain dysfunction have led to extraordinary breakthroughs, especially in the area of reading. A sizable body of evidence indicates that poor readers exhibit disruption primarily, but not exclusively, in the neural circuitry of the brain's left hemisphere, the part that serves language.[11]

Researchers are now beginning to conclude that there is some disruption in the neural circuitry in the brain of a disabled reader that explains their difficulty.

In addition to these imaging studies, brain research at the Dyslexia Research Laboratory at Beth Israel Deaconess Medical Center in Boston indicates anatomical differences between the nondyslexic and dyslexic brains. The outer layers of the brains of people with dyslexia contain unusual clusters of neurons, called ectopias, which formed in utero where brain cells that would normally be in a central part of the brain migrated too far out into a section of the outer cortex. These ectopias are believed to alter the connecting pathways between the different processing areas of the brain. Neuroscientists have also discovered that important auditory centers in the left and right hemispheres of the brain of a person with dyslexia are more closely equal in size than those of non-dyslexic individuals, whose left auditory centers are larger than their right centers.[12]

Brain anatomy and functional imaging research is of great interest to many people who have worked with children with dyslexia. Tutors and special education teachers often report that reading is a fundamentally different and difficult task for a person with dyslexia, and it has been validating for them to see that the problems they address have a neurological basis. The findings of neuroscience increasingly explain the behavioral characteristics of their students. Nevertheless, scientists who are providing basic research are quick to explain that no treatments or therapies that directly alter the brain, aside from teaching itself, have been proven. Structured, step-by-step practice is still the best treatment for the condition.

Research scientists are pursuing studies of brain plasticity and the critical periods for fostering brain development. Questions abound. To what extent is it possible to change the pathways in a brain through stimulation so that an injury or developmental learning problem can be overcome? Does intensive intervention at an early age actually change the way the brain processes sounds or print? Currently, researchers are comparing brain images of children with dyslexia before and after intensive instruction in reading using a multisensory structured language remediation approach.

Would all children who experience difficulty in learning to read or spell be considered dyslexic?

Within the field of reading psychology there has been no clear agreement about which of the children who experience some difficulty in learning to read would be considered dyslexic. That is because reading difficulty exists on a continuum of severity, individual expression of the disorder varies, and the symptoms change over time, depending on the kind of education that a person receives. Reading ability, like height, weight, intelligence, and running speed, is distributed according to the normal (bell) curve, with some children having difficulty, some children finding the process really easy, and most children somewhere in between these two ends of the spectrum. For research purposes, scientists usually draw the line at the 20th or 30th percentile to classify a child as a poor reader. There is no special cluster of children at the lower end of the distribution who are easy to identify.

The determination of the proper label for children is of more than passing interest because several states, such as Texas and Louisiana, provide services for children with dyslexia under laws that are separate from special education laws. One difficulty in distinguishing groups of children, however, is that many show difficulties with phonological processing, language, or print awareness that are the consequence of poor instruction or lack of opportunity to learn. In essence, many children fail to learn because their problems are not caught early or addressed aggressively, and they end up being indistinguishable from children who have had every opportunity to learn but who have not succeeded. The first type of child is actually more common and is known by researchers as the "garden-variety poor reader." The second type of child is the one who more justifiably deserves the classification "dyslexic." If we compare the number of children who are poor readers (25 percent) with the number who remain poor readers even if they are intensively and appropriately taught (5 percent), we can estimate that about 20 percent show dyslexic-like symptoms that are readily treatable.

The determination of dyslexia is also complicated by the fact that good instruction produces good results and that the symptoms of the disorder change over time. If a person succeeds at learning to read, her problems will be more evident in the form of slow reading, poor spelling, difficulty with writing, and difficulty in learning the grammar, spelling, and pronunciation of a foreign language. She may score in the average range in the ability to read words, especially if the test is untimed, but she will still show problems with phonological processing and will still make errors that are uncommon for nondyslexic people.

How Symptoms of Dyslexia Change over Time

Grade Span	Typical Symptoms
K–2	Trouble segmenting and blending speech sounds.
	Poor letter-sound memory and recall.
	Poor application of phonics while reading.
	Inconsistent memory for "sight" words.
	Trouble remembering lists such as the months of the year.
	Mispronunciation of words.
	Inability to spell phonetically.
3–4	Slow and/or inaccurate phonic decoding.
	Inconsistent word recognition. *cont.*

Poor spelling; misrepresentation of speech sounds.

Overreliance on context and guessing while reading.

Trouble learning new vocabulary words (spoken).

Confusion about other symbols, such as math operation signs.

5–6 Poor spelling; poor punctuation.

Reversion to manuscript from cursive.

Poor organization of writing.

Laborious decoding of words; skipping unknown words.

Avoidance of reading.

7–8 Slow reading; loss of meaning.

Persistent problems with distinguishing similar words.

Poor spelling and writing; inaccurate spelling of speech sounds.

Poor recall or identification of letter sequences.

Better performance with explicit, systematic, structured teaching of language.

9+ Trouble with foreign language grammar and vocabulary.

Continuation of writing and spelling problems.

Slow and labored reading; inability to sustain effort.

High degree of difficulty with longer writing assignments.

Better performance when given extra time, study strategies, and structured language teaching.

The good news from research into the treatment of reading disabilities is that reading, spelling, and phonological problems respond to similar treatment regardless of the cause. The child needs more explicit instruction in phonemic awareness, systematic phonics, and the application of reading skills to reading books. The child whose deficit was caused by insufficient instruction is more likely to catch up and overcome the problem with capable teaching. If instruction has been well designed and well delivered and the child is still not learning, then it is likely that a learning disability is present. Such children need to be evaluated and often benefit from explicit and intensive intervention carried out individually or in small groups.

What are some warning signs of a learning disability?

The Coordinated Campaign for Learning Disabilities, a consortium of six organizations that provides information about learning disabilities, offers this list of common warning signs:

Early Warning Signs of a Learning Disability
(from the Coordinated Campaign for Learning Disabilities)

Preschool
- Late talking, compared to other children.
- Pronunciation problems.
- Slow vocabulary growth; often unable to find the right word.

K to Fourth Grade
- Slow to learn the connection between letters and sounds.
- Confusion of basic words (*run, eat, want*).

cont.

- Difficulty in learning numbers, the alphabet, days of the week.
- Extremely restless and easily distracted.
- Trouble interacting with peers.
- Poor ability to follow directions or routines.

- Multiple reading and spelling errors, including letter reversal (b/d), inversions (m/w), transpositions (felt/left), and substitutions (house/home).
- Transposition of number sequences and confusion of arithmetic signs (+, −, /, =).
- Slow recall of facts.
- Slow to learn new skills; heavy reliance on memorization.
- Impulsiveness; lack of planning.
- Unstable pencil grip.
- Trouble learning about time.
- Poor coordination; unaware of physical surroundings; prone to accidents.

Current diagnostic procedures are dependent on careful observation of the child's successes and difficulties in learning. A parent's extensive knowledge of a child's growth patterns and the child's strengths and weaknesses should be attended to in the evaluation process. The parent plays a significant and special role in helping to identify the nature and origins of a learning problem.

Not all children who begin to lag behind their peers in learning to read are in trouble. Some children do get off to a slow start and then catch up. After all, most children need three or four years of instruction before they are proficient enough to read for information on their own. The key is to know when you have enough data points that, when taken together, add up to the probability of a learning disability and the need to take action.

The following list of benchmark reading accomplishments for kindergarten to third grade was included in a report prepared by a National Academy of Sciences panel titled *Preventing Reading Difficulties in Young Children.*[13]

Benchmarks in Reading Accomplishments
(from *Preventing Reading Difficulties in Young Children*)

Kindergarten Accomplishments
- Knows the parts of a book and their functions.
- Begins to track print when listening to a familiar text being read or when rereading own writing.
- "Reads" familiar texts emergently, i.e., not necessarily verbatim from the print alone.
- Recognizes and can name all uppercase and lowercase letters.
- Understands that the sequence of letters in a written word represents the sequence of sounds (phonemes) in a spoken word (alphabetic principle).
- Learns many, though not all, one-to-one letter-sound correspondences.
- Recognizes some words by sight, including a few very common ones (*a, the, I, my, you, is, are*).   *cont.*

- Uses new vocabulary and grammatical constructions in own speech.
- Makes appropriate switches from oral to written language situations.
- Notices when simple sentences fail to make sense.
- Connects information and events in texts to life, and life to text experiences.
- Retells, reenacts, or dramatizes stories or parts of stories.
- Listens attentively to books teacher reads to class.
- Can name some book titles and authors.
- Demonstrates familiarity with a number of types or genres of text (e.g., storybooks, expository texts, poems, newspapers, and everyday print such as signs, notices, labels).
- Correctly answers questions about stories read aloud.
- Makes predictions based on illustrations or portions of stories.
- Demonstrates understanding that spoken words consist of a sequence of phonemes.
- Given spoken sets like "dan, dan, den," can identify the first two as being the same and the third as different.
- Given spoken sets like "dak, pat, zen," can identify the first two as sharing a same sound.
- Given spoken segments, can merge them into a meaningful target word.
- Given a spoken word, can produce another word that rhymes with it.
- Independently writes many uppercase and lowercase letters.
- Uses phonemic awareness and letter knowledge to spell independently (invented or creative spelling).
- Writes (unconventionally) to express own meaning.   *cont.*

- Builds a repertoire of some conventionally spelled words.
- Shows awareness of distinction between "kid writing" and conventional orthography.
- Writes own name (first and last) and the first names of some friends or classmates.
- Can write most letters and some words when they are dictated.

First-Grade Accomplishments

- Makes a transition from emergent to "real" reading.
- Reads aloud with accuracy and comprehension any text that is appropriately designed for the first half of grade 1.
- Accurately decodes orthographically regular one-syllable words and nonsense words (e.g., *sit, zot),* using print-sound mappings to sound out unknown words.
- Uses letter-sound correspondence knowledge to sound out unknown words when reading text.
- Recognizes common, irregularly spelled words by sight *(have, said, where, two).*
- Has a reading vocabulary of 300 to 500 words, sight words, and easily sounded-out words.
- Monitors own reading and self-corrects when an incorrectly identified word does not fit with cues provided by the letters in the word or the context surrounding the word.
- Reads and comprehends both fiction and nonfiction that are appropriately designed for grade level.
- Shows evidence of expanding language repertory, including increasing appropriate use of standard, more formal language registers. *cont.*

- Creates own written texts for others to read.
- Notices when difficulties are encountered in understanding text.
- Reads and understands simple written instructions.
- Predicts and justifies what will happen next in stories.
- Discusses prior knowledge of topics in expository texts.
- Discusses how, why, and what-if questions in sharing nonfiction texts.
- Describes new information gained from texts in own words.
- Distinguishes whether simple sentences are incomplete or fail to make sense; notices when simple texts fail to make sense.
- Can answer simple written comprehension questions based on material read.
- Can count the number of syllables in a word.
- Can blend or segment the phonemes of most one-syllable words.
- Spells correctly three- and four-letter short-vowel words.
- Composes fairly readable first drafts using appropriate parts of the writing process (some attention to planning, drafting, rereading for meaning, and some self-correction).
- Uses invented spelling/phonics-based knowledge to spell independently, when necessary.
- Shows spelling consciousness or sensitivity to conventional spelling.
- Uses basic punctuation and capitalization.
- Produces a variety of types of compositions (e.g., stories, descriptions, journal entries), showing appropriate relationships between printed text, illustrations, and other graphics.
- Engages in a variety of literary activities voluntarily (e.g., choosing books and stories to read, writing a note to a friend).

cont.

Second-Grade Accomplishments

- Reads and comprehends both fiction and nonfiction that are appropriately designed for grade level.
- Accurately decodes orthographically regular multisyllable words and nonsense words (e.g., *capital, Kalamazoo).*
- Uses knowledge of print-sound mappings to sound out unknown words.
- Accurately reads many irregularly spelled words and such spelling patterns as diphthongs, special vowel spellings, and common word endings.
- Shows evidence of expanding language repertory, including increasing use of more formal language registers.
- Reads voluntarily for interest and own purposes.
- Rereads sentences when meaning is not clear.
- Interprets information from diagrams, charts, and graphs.
- Recalls facts and details of texts.
- Reads nonfiction materials for answers to specific questions or for specific purposes.
- Takes part in creative responses to texts such as dramatizations, oral presentations, fantasy play, etc.
- Discusses similarities in characters and events across stories.
- Connects and compares information across nonfiction selections.
- Poses possible answers to how, why, and what-if questions.
- Correctly spells previously studied words and spelling patterns in own writing.
- Represents the complete sound of a word when spelling independently.

cont.

- Shows sensitivity to using formal language patterns in place of oral language patterns at appropriate spots in own writing (e.g., decontextualizing sentences, conventions for quoted speech, literary language forms, proper verb forms).
- Makes reasonable judgments about what to include in written products.
- Productively discusses ways to clarify and refine writing of own and others.
- With assistance, adds use of conferencing, revision, and editing processes to clarify and refine own writing to the steps of the expected parts of the writing process.
- Given organizational help, writes informative well-structured reports.
- Attends to spelling, mechanics, and presentation for final products.
- Produces a variety of types of compositions (e.g., stories, reports, correspondence).

Third-Grade Accomplishments
- Reads aloud with fluency and comprehension any test that is appropriately designed for grade level.
- Uses letter-sound correspondence knowledge and structural analysis to decode words.
- Reads and comprehends both fiction and nonfiction that are appropriately designed for grade level.
- Reads longer fictional selections and chapter books independently.
- Takes part in creative responses to texts such as dramatizations, oral presentations, fantasy play, etc.   *cont.*

- Can point to or clearly identify specific words or wordings that are causing comprehension difficulties.
- Summarizes major points from fiction and nonfiction texts.
- In interpreting fiction, discusses underlying theme or message.
- Asks how, why, and what-if questions in interpreting nonfiction texts.
- In interpreting nonfiction, distinguishes cause and effect, fact and opinion, main idea and supporting details.
- Uses information and reasoning to examine bases of hypotheses and opinions.
- Infers word meanings from taught roots, prefixes, and suffixes.
- Correctly spells previously studied words and spelling patterns in own writing.
- Begins to incorporate literacy words and language patterns in own writing (e.g., elaborates descriptions, uses figurative wording).
- With some guidance, uses all aspects of the writing process in producing own compositions and reports.
- Combines information from multiple sources in writing reports.
- With assistance, suggests and implements editing and revision to clarify and refine own writing.
- Presents and discusses own writing with other students and responds helpfully to other students' compositions.
- Independently reviews work for spelling, mechanics, and presentation.
- Produces a variety of written works (e.g., literature responses, reports, "published" books, semantic maps) in a variety of formats, including multimedia forms.

Even thinking about the possibility of a learning disability makes me feel scared. How do I deal with this?

It is natural for conscientious parents to be anxious and uncertain if their children run into learning difficulties. As they learn more, adults may discover that undiagnosed learning disabilities, similar to those that are affecting the children, run in their family. Adults may remember having difficulty in school; however, the term "learning disability" was not even formulated until the late 1960s, and very few contemporary parents were diagnosed with a learning disorder as a child.

In previous generations people toughed out their problems. They may have gotten through school with a few paddlings for misspelling or reading badly, a few lectures on their character flaws, or an early departure from school. People who made it through school might have gravitated toward fields where they excelled, and avoided fields that required strong skills in their areas of weakness. Successful engineers, designers, farmers, or political leaders could dictate to their office helpers or spouses. Therefore, many of you will be the first in your extended families to discover or acknowledge a long-standing family condition.

Susan had absolutely no knowledge about learning disabilities eight years ago. She began to suspect that her son's difficulty in learning to read was something other than a developmental lag. It caught her completely off guard because no one in either her husband's or her family had ever been diagnosed with LD before her son was diagnosed as dyslexic. She remembers during the first three months of their journey that she was hesitant to discuss her concerns with any of her friends because she felt that learning disabilities meant being pulled out for special education and she was worried about her child's self-esteem. If only she had called the one friend she knew who had a child in special education at her school. She would have referred her to the best diagnostician in their area, and Susan would have saved months of time and quite a bit of money. Instead she followed a more confidential (and less informed) referral source. Often fellow parents can give you the best advice.

On the positive side, Louisa repeatedly looks to her family history to understand and have patience with the difficulties of her child. There is some relief in being able to say, "She's a chip off the old block—fulfilling her destiny!" She may never enjoy reading, but many of her successful relatives are in walks of life that minimize reading and writing.

Even though it feels scary at first, it is absolutely critical that parents cope with their fears and move along quickly in their journey toward obtaining appropriate help. In Chapter 1 we mentioned the Roper Poll that the CCLD commissioned to determine the level of public awareness about learning disabilities. One of the most troubling results of this 1999 survey of seventeen hundred people is that parents are reluctant to take action quickly enough if they suspect their child has a learning disability. The CCLD believes that parents adopt a wait-and-see attitude because of their fear of being stigmatized by family, friends, or teachers. The poll shows that nearly half of parents (48 percent) feel that having their child labeled "learning-disabled" is more harmful than struggling with the problem privately. An alarming 44 percent of parents who considered that their child might have a learning problem waited for the child to exhibit signs of difficulty for a year or more before they acknowledged a problem.[14]

How does the school identify a child who is struggling in learning to read?

Each school has its own approach to identifying children who need help, although those practices are typically governed by state law and district policy. We can't tell you what you will find in your child's school, but we can share with you some models of how children are identified based on our experience in working with many different schools over many years. Some of the things you want to be concerned about are:

- How children's needs are identified.
- What kind of help is offered.
- What intensity of help is offered.
- How long the help continues.
- How progress is measured.

Again, early identification and intervention are critical. You should be sure that the instruction given is an approach supported by research and known to other reputable experts. You must be certain that the person delivering the instruction has been properly trained in that method. Your goal is to let the school offer a program, monitor the effectiveness of it, and then advocate for a different kind of help if the program is not working as it should. Allowing your child to continue with the school's intervention approach if she isn't making sufficient progress is often a mistake.

You also want to make sure that your school is using one of the validated early reading inventories to identify children at risk for reading difficulty in kindergarten and first grade. Until recently, schools viewed first grade as a developmental year when reading instruction was provided. If children had reading problems, they were passed on to second grade with the hope that they would catch up, or they were repeated in first grade for more of the same instruction. These practices have caused the third and fourth grades to be peak years for identification of learning disabilities and referrals to remedial reading.

Educational policies have discouraged early identification of children. Until recently, it was common for teachers to be advised by a school administrator to avoid referring children for testing until they were at least a year behind. Many school districts wait for a child to be not one year behind, but two years behind, before assessment is undertaken. Principals used to view this "year behind" guideline as a way of conserving their valuable testing budget. The longer the school waits, the more clear it will be which students have problems because the spread between their performance and their grade level will be wider. To us this is a clear case of educational malpractice. Fortunately, more and more schools are adopting a proactive approach to identifying students at risk for difficulty and offering help before they fail.

There are different types of help that can be obtained before you commit to having your child evaluated. The classroom teacher may provide extra help within the classroom, sometimes even before mentioning to you that she is worried about your child's lack of progress. She can deliver instruction that she feels fits with your child's needs by placing your child in a particular reading group and working on different skills with that group. Sometimes there is an assistant teacher or aide in the classroom who will either work with the struggling group or free up the teacher so she can work with them. The small-group instruction is most likely to work well if it follows a validated instructional sequence and uses proven methods such as Project Read, Read Well, or Alphabetic Phonics.

Many teachers hesitate to mention their concerns about a child's reading progress to the parents. Their underlying reason is usually good—they don't want to alarm you. Many teachers want to try on their own to solve a child's learning problem before bringing it up to a parent, especially if they have had success before with another student. The teacher may also want to prevent the transfer of parental anxiety to the child, who is already insecure and eager to please. In the long run, however, it is more helpful to keep parents informed as concerns develop, and to involve them in the process of figuring out what is going on with the child.

What is a school likely to do with a first grader who is behind in reading?

Some schools have reading specialists who begin working with first-grade students right away if they fail a screening. Some provide a tutor immediately. Some teachers regroup children according to ability and make sure they get at least ninety minutes of instruction.

If your classroom teacher offers to help your child, you need to ask some questions and document the answers.

Questions to Ask Your Child's Teacher
When Extra Reading Help Is Offered

- Will the help be provided by a paraprofessional, volunteer, or trained teacher?
- What specific approach is being used?
- What kind of training in the approach has the instructor had?
- What will the child miss in the classroom while she gets this help?
- Where will my child receive this help and with what other students?
- Can I come and watch a session?

In some schools parents are trained to work as volunteers to help students. If your family has a history of dyslexia, or you suspect a more severe problem than the school is acknowledging, then you will probably want to decline any help that is not from a highly trained academic therapist or reading expert. A child with genuine difficulties will need instruction delivered by an experienced expert using an effective method for sufficient time for the child to catch up to grade level.

Once a child is struggling in reading, who determines that she needs to be tested?

Within the school system the decision to test a child is usually made by the classroom teacher and the principal. If a reading specialist has been working with your child, he or she might also provide a recommendation. Requests for testing can also come from parents. You need to put your request in writing, probably to the principal, and you need to say in your letter that you are concerned that your child might have a learning disability. The school is not required to test your child just because you request it. They can deny testing unless they, too, believe there are reasons to suspect a learning disability. However, if you have any concerns, it is always advisable to make your request, and always put it in writing. A school district that continues to deny testing when a parent has documented repeated requests will look bad in a hearing later if the parent is proved right and the school obstructed a referral for testing. Most schools yield to legitimate parental pressure for testing, unless they have solid evidence that the child is, in fact, doing well in school.

If the school decides not to test your child and you have the financial means to test her outside school, it may be wise to proceed independently just to save time. Exhaust the resources at school first, but take action when time is passing without resolution of your concern.

chapter 5

Having Your Child Tested

Though my seven-year-old son is doing well in school, reading still seems to be difficult for him. I would like to have him tested to see if there are any weak areas that could be strengthened. We have several commercial learning centers in our area, but are they the correct place to have him evaluated? Are there specific tests that you would recommend?

This parent is asking a common question. Parents can choose from several testing options, and each type of testing has a specific purpose and outcome. There are many different levels of assessment—from seeking an informal screening by an experienced teacher, to an assessment based on a full assortment of tests known as psychoeducational or neuropsychological testing. You will get the best results if you are clear about *why* you are seeking testing, what you want to know, and what you will do with the information once the testing is completed. As you develop answers to these questions, you can deliberately choose not only the right scope and manner of testing but also the right person to do the testing.

This chapter will be organized around four important questions about testing:

- *Why.* What are your concerns, and what information are you seeking?
- *What level of testing.* What is the appropriate level of assessment?
- *When.* When is the opportune time for testing?
- *Who.* How can you select an appropriate evaluator who is qualified to do the level of testing you have selected?

Why do you want to have your child tested?

The reasons parents seek testing of their child are as diverse as the types of difficulties children may experience. Children are tested to determine if they are behind grade level, to confirm a suspicion of a learning disability, to verify that a child has the same learning disability as his sibling or parent, to determine what kind of help a child might need, or to measure progress toward a goal. All of these are valid reasons to decide to have your child tested, but the reasons for testing should determine what type of testing to do. Unfortunately, many parents believe that there is only one type of testing, so they unknowingly choose comprehensive psychoeducational testing when a briefer test battery would be sufficient for understanding a problem and what to do about it. Often parents could determine what they need to know from a brief, focused assessment, but instead contract for comprehensive testing because they believe that they would not be able to get any help for their child without it.

Parents who make wise choices about testing their child are able to do so because they are clear about what they hope to accomplish from the testing. The first questions to ask are:

- What are my concerns, and can I define them clearly?
- What questions am I trying to answer?
- What do I hope to accomplish with testing?
- What decisions am I trying to make with the results of the testing?

Any parent who has lived for several years with a diffuse, undefined feeling that something is wrong is understandably feeling anxious to confirm suspicions or allay concerns. Parents' observations are usually on target when it comes to identifying a learning disability or other educational problem. However, you need to resist the temptation to jump into testing before you clarify what you are trying to accomplish. Testing will not answer all of your questions, such as whether your child will be able to attend college. Some qualities you want to know more about, such as creativity, leadership character traits, and artistic talent, will not be directly measured in an assessment. Evaluators can answer certain questions about children's development better than others.

In addition, the timing for an assessment should be carefully chosen: children are most reliably and purposefully evaluated when their lives are relatively stable and when a major transition is ahead, such as entry into a new school, or making a commitment to summer tutoring. Testing is more meaningful at certain ages; for example, it is easier to measure the effects of an attention problem after the child has been in school long enough to be adjusted to routines and expectations of the classroom. If parents seek a complete psychoeducational or neuropsychological evaluation from a qualified evaluator, some specific preparation should be done to ensure that the most benefit is obtained from the experience, which is both costly and time-consuming.

What do you want from the testing?

Psychologists and other evaluators can be most efficient when the person making the referral has formulated a clear question. The more specific the information you give the evaluator, the better. In fact, any insurance company that helps pay for an evaluation will ask immediately for a statement of the referral question. An example of a good referral question is this:

> Mark at mid-first grade is unable to successfully read grade-level material. He recognizes only about a third of the approximately one hundred sight words the class has been working on since the beginning of the school year. When he reaches an unknown word, he is unable to sound out anything but the first consonant, which he only gets right about half the time. He has difficulty with rhyming. He doesn't seem to remember his sounds. He has excellent oral language skills and understands everything I read aloud to him and seems to be very curious about the information contained in books. He wants to learn to read, but it is frustrating for him and he would rather have me do it. I suspect that his knowledge of the letter-sound correspondences is weak. What do you think is causing his difficulty with reading?

This explicit referral question gives enough information that the evaluator can immediately begin thinking about what tests to give and what other questions to ask of the parents. A good evaluator will vary the specific tests used in an assessment in accordance with the child's age and the referral question.

Evaluation done during the preschool years can and should include speech and language assessment. Any preschooler suspected of having language delays or language difficulty, and any older child reported to have language deficits, should be assessed by a speech and language specialist. Preschool children with speech or language delays are very much at risk for developing reading problems unless they are well taught. If your preschool child has unusual difficulties with making himself understood by adults, pronouncing speech sounds, learning words, or interpreting what is said to him, contact the school district immediately to ask what age they begin screening children. Most school districts offer free speech and language screening for children who are three and four years old. If your child is not within normal limits on early speech screening, the therapist may recommend your child for an intervention program or suggest that he be followed and reevaluated. At the very least, the therapist will give you games and activities to do at home that can improve your child's language.

What is psychoeducational testing?

The terms for tests can be confusing to parents. The term "psychoeducational" does not mean that the child's personality, family relationships, or emotional state is necessarily going to be assessed. Psychoeducational testing entails a full battery of tests that are designed to measure cognitive ability

(IQ), academic achievement in different areas, language proficiency, and some nonacademic processes that are related to learning, such as the ability to copy symbols quickly or remember lists of numbers. A skilled evaluator must select which tests, both formal and informal, are most likely to pinpoint weaknesses and illuminate strengths.

What should you expect if you do have a specialist evaluate your child? Typically, an evaluator or psychologist obtains a family history and will talk to you and your child before conducting any standardized tests. A good evaluator will give a few major tests first and then choose what additional testing may be necessary to illuminate and document the nature of the child's problem. Evaluators and psychologists almost always give an IQ test such as the WISC-III (Wechsler Intelligence Scale for Children—III) or the Stanford-Binet—IV, both of which are designed to estimate the child's problem-solving and reasoning abilities. IQ tests given individually do not require the child to read; thus, those who cannot read may still shine in general reasoning and problem-solving skills. IQ tests are typically divided into language (verbal) and nonlanguage (performance) areas, with a composite score for each area. Evaluators should also always give several reliable measures of academic performance, or achievement, in the area of concern.

After conducting the ability and achievement tests, the evaluator usually determines which additional, more specialized, tests to give. The evaluator determines these tests by developing hypotheses about the nature of the child's problem while observing his strengths and weaknesses during the IQ and achievement tests. After delivering about five to ten shorter, well-selected tests of various functions related to the problem, a knowledgeable evaluator is able to determine which of the more specialized tests will provide the most enlightening information. For example, if the child is having trouble reading fluently, the evaluator might give more timed tests of letter memory, naming, and recall in order to see if there is a fundamental problem with the speed dimension of memory. Certainly, a timed oral reading and a timed silent reading measure would be appropriate.

On average, the testing takes three to five hours. The evaluator will then prepare a written report summarizing the test scores and his/her interpretation of them, including a diagnosis if one is justified, and recommend a plan to address the issues. Typically, the evaluator meets with the parents to explain the results and go over the written report.

In a good psychoeducational test the evaluator is trying to accomplish five goals:

1. Answer the referral question.
2. Establish whether your child qualifies for special services of any kind under state laws because of a learning disability or other impairment.
3. Classify and describe the specific type of learning disability or difficulty.
4. Make well-reasoned recommendations for instructional programs and methods that should help.
5. Provide advice on any special accommodations that will maximize the child's ability to learn, such as extra timing on tests, special equipment, preferential classroom seating, or special instructions.

It takes an experienced, well-trained evaluator with specialized knowledge of psychology, language, education, and education regulations to accomplish all of these goals in a three-to-five-hour assessment. Many evaluators can meet some, but not all, of these goals, and true experts with broad knowledge who can also relate well to adults and children are fairly hard to find.

How does the evaluator determine whether a child is dyslexic?

There is no "dyslexia test battery" to diagnose dyslexia. In fact, there is no single, approved test battery to determine whether a child has any other specific learning disability or attention deficit disorder (ADD). Since there is no single test to diagnose dyslexia, the psychologist or evaluator must piece together information from many of the subtests of standardized tests, along with information gathered from less formal assessments. The same diagnosis may be made by two qualified evaluators using different test batteries.

Many evaluators are directed by state or federal policies to measure the difference between intellectual ability (IQ) and level of academic achievement. A "significant discrepancy" between ability and achievement qualifies a child for special services under the category "learning disability." The discrepancy is often reported in terms of standard scores and standard deviations, statistical concepts that measure the degree to which a discrepancy between intellectual ability and achievement is large or unusual. In most states the discrepancy must be 1, 1.5, or 2 standard deviations to qualify a student for special services. In addition to requiring documentation of a discrepancy between IQ and achievement, some states require documentation of a "processing deficit" to verify that a student's achievement problem is not due to motivational issues, lack of school attendance, or poor teaching. Most also require that the need for special education be well documented.

Only recently have scientists offered solid evidence that the discrepancy requirement for an LD classification is a questionable and even wasteful practice. Researchers recommend that conditions such as dyslexia be identified on the basis of specific language processing symptoms. "Dyslexia" may be an appropriate diagnostic term when an individual is having trouble learning specific language, reading, and spelling skills in spite of adequate instruction and adequate intellectual ability. Leading researchers such as Keith Stanovich, Linda Siegel, and Jack Fletcher have recommended that discrepancy between IQ and achievement is not relevant to identifying a reading problem, but our educational policies have yet to catch up with scientific thinking.

Another issue is that obtaining a large enough discrepancy between IQ and achievement may qualify the child as learning-disabled, but a discrepancy is not a diagnosis. The evaluator must be able to explain *why* that discrepancy is there. More important, even if there is no discrepancy between ability and achievement scores, evaluators must be able to look at how well the child performs specific reading, spelling, writing, and language tasks. The evaluator should know the research on reading and reading problems.

The International Dyslexia Association distributes a booklet that provides an overview of the testing process, including information about the wide variety of assessments that should be included in the process. From this information, we constructed the following table:[1]

Components of Testing to Assess Dyslexia
(Specific Language-Based Reading Disability)

Category	*Includes*
Family and individual history	• Other family members who had difficulty with learning to speak, read, write, and spell. • Health or medical impairments to learning. • Any delays in developing spoken language in preschool. • Parents' concern about speech, language, motor skills, or attention span.
Cognitive ability or intellectual aptitude (IQ) (now considered optional)	• Either a Wechsler (WISC-III, WAIS-III) or Stanford-Binet IQ test; possibly the Woodcock-Johnson Test of Cognitive Abilities. Test should measure individual's aptitude for learning in verbal, logical, mathematical, visual-motor, visual-spatial, symbolic, memory, and attentional domains.
Specific language skills	• Speech sound and syllable awareness. • Word pronunciation. • Word retrieval. • Rapid naming of letters, numbers, colors, objects. • Knowledge of word meanings. *cont.*

- Comprehension and production of sentence structure (syntax).
- Expressive verbal ability, including organization of ideas, elaboration, and clarity of expression.
- Comprehension of what is heard and read.

Single-word decoding and reading fluency	• Ability to read single words out of context under timed and untimed conditions. • Ability to apply phonic word attack to reading nonsense words, timed and untimed. • Oral paragraph reading fluency and accuracy.
Reading comprehension	• Timed readings of longer passages read silently. • Ability to summarize, answer multiple choice questions, or complete cloze tasks (i.e., fill in the blanks).
Spelling	• Dictated spelling test (not multiple choice). • Developmental spelling inventory. • Analysis of errors for speech sound omission, letter sequence confusion, and poor memory for common words.

cont.

Written comprehension	• Composition of a story or essay for students capable of writing more than a few sentences. • Analysis of word choice, conceptual organization, sentence quality, elaboration of ideas, grammar, and use of punctuation and capitalization. • Informal tasks such as writing a paraphrase, combining simple sentences into compound and complex sentences, writing an outline and summary of a passage, or writing part of a structured paragraph.
Handwriting	• Ability to form letters, both alone and in words. • Analysis of writing to see if it sits consistently on the baseline. • Consistency and slant of letters. • Right- or left-handed. • Appropriate pencil grip. • Appropriate rotation of paper.

There are many different tests that assess the same skill, and there are some minor differences among the tests in a given category. Most evaluators prefer one test among the several available and tend to use that test most frequently. The most commonly used assessment tools are as follows:

Assessment of Reading Difficulty, Tests Commonly Used

Area of Functioning	Specific Skill to Test	Commonly Used Tests
Reading words	*Letter and Word Decoding* • Real words in lists • Nonsense words in lists • Knowledge of phonic associations • Decoding new words in context *Reading Whole Words* • High-frequency sight words	• Woodcock Reading Mastery Test • Woodcock-Johnson Psychoeducational Battery—3 • Wechsler Individual Achievement Test • Test of Word Reading Efficiency • Decoding Skills Test • Kaufman Test of Educational Achievement
Pre-reading skills	*Phonemic Awareness and Alphabet Knowledge* • Rhyming, blending, segmenting, identifying syllables and speech sounds	• Lindamood Auditory *Conceptualization Test* • Rosner Test of Auditory Analysis Skills • Torgesen-Bryant Test of Phonological Awareness (TOPA) • Test of Phonological Awareness (LinguiSystems) • Comprehensive Test of Phonological Processing • Slingerland Screening Test • Texas Primary Reading Inventory (TPRI) • Fox in a Box

cont.

Reading fluency and comprehension	*Oral Reading*	• Gray Oral Reading Test—3 • Informal Reading Inventory
	Silent Reading Comprehension	• Woodcock-Johnson Passage Reading • Nelson-Denny (for adolescents) • Wechsler Individual Achievement Test • Kaufman Test of Educational Achievement
Spelling	*Writing Words to Dictation*	• Test of Written Spelling—4 • Wide Range Achievement Test—3 • Qualitative Inventory of Spelling Development
	Spelling Words in Writing	• Analysis of written compositions
Oral language skills	*Listening Comprehension* • Word knowledge • Understanding sentence structure • Passage or paragraph understanding	• Test of Language Development • Test of Adolescent Language • Clinical Evaluation of Language Fundamentals
	Expressive Language • Speed of naming • Sentence production • Describing and summarizing	• Test of Word Knowledge • Rapid Automatic Naming • Wechsler Individual Achievement Test
Writing	*Composing a Story or Narrative*	• Test of Written Language • Wechsler Individual Achievement Test <div align="right">*cont.*</div>

	Knowledge of Symbolic Conventions	• Test of Written Language • Test of Written Expression • Woodcock-Johnson
Intellectual ability	*Verbal and Nonverbal Reasoning*	• Wechsler Intelligence Scale for Children—III • Stanford-Binet—IV • Woodcock-Johnson Test of Cognitive Abilities
Visual-motor skills	*Form Copying*	• Bender Gestalt Test • Visual Motor Integration Test • Rey Complex Figure Drawing
	Writing	• Slingerland Screening Test

Do I need to do anything to prepare for testing?

At the beginning of fourth grade my son was only able to read eleven out of twenty words in isolation on a third-grade word list. He often looks at the beginning of the word and guesses what the word is without really decoding it. Often he is wrong. For example, he would read *instead* as *inside, shut* as *shout,* and *ruin* as *rain.* Now he is entering fifth grade and recently tested in the sixteenth percentile for overall reading of passages. I believe his writing is below average, also. If you ask him just to get his ideas down on paper, about 50 percent of the words are misspelled. He uses his analytical skills to comprehend what he is reading, yet it will take him so much longer to read something than it seems like it should.

This mother has pinpointed her questions extremely well. She has collected concrete quantifiable data about her areas of concern. She can tell the evaluator not only her son's scores on the subtests of the standardized tests performed in school but also some anecdotal information about her son's spelling and reading errors. Data of this sort are valuable in the initial meeting with the person who will be testing your child.

Information to Provide to an Evaluator

- Selected spelling tests and current spelling lists from school.
- Writing samples, especially first drafts rather than the final edited version.
- Samples of books that your child is currently reading.
- List of words that your child frequently mispronounces.
- All standardized tests from school.
- Any previous testing done by another evaluator, including the written reports.
- Medical records and information about hearing or vision problems.
- Development milestones such as when your child talked in full sentences.
- Notes about which of the warning signs of a learning disability you observe regularly.
- Comments or concerns expressed by teachers or other informed professionals.
- Information about the type of reading instruction your child has received so far.

What are the different levels of testing?

Let's take a look at three levels of testing—quick, specialized, and full—and compare and contrast the information you will receive and how much each will cost.

LEVEL 1: Quick Assessment

The least expensive and time-consuming assessment is done by an experienced reading or language therapist (tutor) who specializes in reading. In an hour or two she can give you a good portrait of your child's instructional needs. A language therapist can usually determine if more testing is advisable. Assuming that you select a language therapist who is experienced in one of the multisensory structured language (MSL) approaches, you may learn the following:

- Whether your child is behind his grade level.
- Whether you should take any further steps at this time.
- What strategies your child uses in decoding (sounding words out, guessing, context, etc.).
- How strong your child's word attack skills are compared to those of his peers.
- Whether his listening comprehension exceeds his silent-reading comprehension.
- Whether your child can break words into their component speech sounds or blend those sounds together.
- What skills he should be learning at this time.

The cost for this consultation varies depending upon your location. Well-trained MSL therapists are currently charging anywhere from $45 to $95 per hour. The tutors or therapists who charge at the high end of that range tend to work in affluent suburbs of major metropolitan areas. If the therapist spends two hours with your child and gives you informal feedback, you are likely to pay $70 to $150 for this information. If the therapist writes up the results, she will ask to be paid significantly more, as report-writing is time-consuming.

When you call the language therapist, be sure to ask about her training and find out if she is comfortable giving you an opinion about your child's reading or learning problems. Ask if she has the tools to compare your child's ability to an accepted standard using grade-level reading passages and other standardized tests. She may use a reading inventory—it typically contains a series of increasingly difficult passages that are designated by grade level—and other subtests of phonic knowledge, instant word recognition, and spelling. The therapist records the number and type of errors as the child reads each passage aloud. After the child reads the passage, the therapist asks him a set of questions to determine how well he comprehended what he read.

To find a qualified language therapist (many prefer this term to "tutor") or evaluator, call your local branch of the International Dyslexia Association (IDA), Academic Language Therapy Association, or Association of Educational Therapists and ask for a list. For the phone number of your nearest IDA branch, call 1-800-ABC-D123 (1-800-222-3123) or visit *www.interdys.org*.

If you need more testing, it is best to have someone other than a language therapist do it. Language therapists may use tests, but these are generally used for measuring the progress that a student is making. The activity of making a formal diagnosis of a problem requires a higher level of expertise, broader training, and supervised testing experience.

LEVEL 2: Limited Testing of Specific Language Areas

The middle level of assessment involves taking your child to a specialized reading clinic for a language and/or reading assessment that does not include IQ testing or more inclusive neuropsychological testing. Such a clinic is not the same thing as a franchised tutoring center such as Sylvan, but rather a clinic that specializes in helping children with dyslexia and other learning disabilities. For example, Lindamood-Bell Learning Processes centers provide specialized, individual assessment of language functioning. Lindamood-Bell provides teacher training and supervision in school districts and they have thirty-three centers located in cities throughout the United States. In their clinic centers they do an initial assessment of two to three hours with the student, followed by a meeting with the parent to discuss the results. This assessment is well worth the charge of $500 to $600. Typically, the evaluator will conduct about eight to twelve standardized tests, including many on our list of valuable assessment tools. In the initial assessment to evaluate a child who is having trouble reading, Lindamood-Bell clinics will typically evaluate these areas:

Areas Evaluated at a Lindamood-Bell Clinic for Students with Reading Difficulties

Oral language skills	• Receptive oral vocabulary—how well the child understands oral vocabulary. • Expressive oral vocabulary—the child's ability to express word opposites. • Oral language comprehension—the child's ability to analyze verbal absurdities and explain what doesn't make sense, or describe a cause or solution for a problem.
Component skills in reading	• Knowledge of the letters and the sound-letter associations. • Spelling skills using pseudo and real words. • Timed word recognition. • Word attack skills (application of phonics). • Ability to read a passage accurately and fluently. • Comprehension of a passage that the child reads.
Specific functions	• Phoneme awareness. • Ability to follow directions for marking visual material.

Most Lindamood-Bell evaluators are not licensed psychologists or psychometricians, so they do not give IQ tests. Their purpose is to determine the child's strengths and weaknesses in the language processing abilities most important for success in reading, spelling, and language comprehension.

Lindamood-Bell evaluators almost always give the Lindamood Auditory Conceptualization (LAC) Test, a test developed by Patricia and Charles Lindamood for measuring phonemic awareness. The LAC Test measures the individual's ability to judge the identity, number, and order of phonemes (speech sounds) in nonsense words that are given in increasing degrees of difficulty. An easy consonant-vowel-consonant nonsense word is *fol,* whereas a difficult one containing five speech sounds is *flosp.* This test also measures the individual's accuracy in tracking subtle speech sound changes in spoken words, a skill that is particularly important for decoding and spelling the English language. The LAC Test uses colored blocks to represent the sounds in words. Students are asked to change the blocks to show changes in sounds from one syllable to the next. For example:

The evaluator says:	*Order of colored blocks:*
These blocks represent "fol."	blue yellow black
Now change "fol" to "fos."	blue yellow white

By using nonsense words, the test forces the student to rely on his awareness of sounds instead of his knowledge of spelling. Lindamood-Bell's national headquarters is in San Luis Obispo, California (1-800-233-1819, *www.LindamoodBell.com).*

Independent reading clinics that do a similar type of diagnostic assessment may be a little harder to find. The best way to find these clinics is to ask other parents, specialists in related fields, or your local branch of the International Dyslexia Association. Ask as well for a list of recommended psychologists who specialize in LD. When you first call the reading clinic, ask what methods they use in teaching reading. They should cite one of the multisensory systematic structured language (MSL) approaches such as Orton-Gillingham, Wilson, Slingerland, Spalding, Lindamood-Bell, Project Read, *LANGUAGE!*, or Alphabetic Phonics. In addition, the Phono-Graphix approach is popular with many academic language therapists who claim it is direct, efficient, and successful in remediating basic decoding problems. Some clinics have developed their own effective approaches following the instructional principles supported by research.

Next you should ask the clinic or evaluator about what kind of assessments they do. If they only provide instruction and do not provide testing, ask for a recommendation for someone who does diagnostic evaluations.

LEVEL 3: **Full Psychoeducational Testing**

A full psychoeducational testing includes a battery of standardized tests plus some informal (nonstandardized) assessments delivered by a psychologist or person licensed to do psychological testing. As described earlier in this chapter, the selection of which tests to conduct is an important decision and requires a qualified person. Sometimes a team of professionals, including the psychologist and language or reading specialist, collaborates on the evaluation. Before the tests begin you will be asked to complete a detailed questionnaire about the history of the child's development and your observations of his behavior. The questions cover your pregnancy, the child's delivery and medical history, developmental milestones, and any behavior that you are concerned about. Often your child's teacher will complete a questionnaire, too, and sometimes the evaluator will interview the teacher at least by telephone.

A written report of ten to fifteen pages should be provided by the evaluator. This report will include a summary of the concerns expressed by the parents, the child's developmental history, the child's educational and instructional history, tables with the specific scores on all tests given, interpretation of the scores, a diagnosis, and recommendations on instruction and accommodations. Usually, the evaluator will meet with the parents to discuss the test results and recommendations and explain what they mean.

Some evaluators prefer to spend a little time getting acquainted with your child before formal testing is begun; others ease into testing gently, getting to know the child as they start working together. The evaluator will begin with easy, inviting tasks that allow him or her to observe your child's language and motor skills and enable your child to become comfortable with the testing situation and the evaluator.

When my son (Susan's) was tested the first time, we were referred to a psychologist who worked for a nearby school district and did a few evaluations outside of school hours. The testing was done on two consecutive Saturday mornings in a medical office that belonged to someone else. I later realized that we used the wrong evaluator and that my child was not comfortable with the person or the environment. The evaluator not only failed to give us the specific diagnosis of dyslexia but also underestimated our son's IQ by a significant degree.

Three years later when some pieces still didn't make sense,

we had a different psychologist retest our son's IQ. She worked in her own office and spent at least thirty minutes on the floor talking with our son before administering any of the subtests. Our son was so much more comfortable with her style and the environment that he performed much better and his IQ was thirty percentile points over the first testing. When I asked two reputable psychologists which score to believe and how this discrepancy could have happened, they both speculated that if our son was uncomfortable with the first psychologist, he may have been distracted, given up, and not answered the questions that he was uncertain about. The higher score is therefore more likely to be representative, and, in fact, it is more consistent with our son's general learning ability as we observe it at home.

When is the right time for testing?

Earlier in the week, while observing my son's first-grade classroom, I became concerned. When I entered the classroom they were having silent reading time. I noticed he was squirmy and inattentive while pretending to read his book, one that I knew was much too difficult for him. His teacher was setting up the giant version of the same reading book on an easel. The bell rang and the kids all rushed to the reading rug to see who could be in the front row around this giant book. They all wanted to be first to read out loud—everyone except my son. He rushed for the wooden bathroom pass. When he returned and it was his turn to read aloud his eyes stared with a glaze at the giant book on the easel. I later asked his teacher, "Is this how reading is taught?" His teacher confidently assured me he would be sending sight vocabulary words home for kids "like my son" who are struggling. Since the other children seem to be learning to read using this approach, should I just wait to see if this works for him?

The fact that some children are able to learn to read within a specific curriculum does not mean that the curriculum is the best available, that it helps most children learn to read, or that it is right for your child. Some children learn with almost any organized approach to instruction; many others are significantly affected by the approach that is used. The children who learn to read with very little systematic instruction in sounds are "wired for sounds" and are able to pick up phonics intuitively. Others need a more explicit and systematic approach to learning the letter-sound associations and how to blend sounds in words.

A referral for testing or a determination of dyslexia may be premature if a child has simply not been exposed to the kind of instruction that develops decoding and reading skills. First, you should ask the teacher to provide more systematic instruction. If possible, you can hire a tutor who has been trained in a systematic structured language approach. If your family has limited financial resources and a family member is able to teach the child at home, then you can try a phonics supplement or structured reading program that is sold commercially. If, after several months of consistent instruction the child does not improve, then it is time to think about testing.

Products for
Teaching Systematic Phonics at Home

Educator's Publishing Service *www.eps.com*	A publishing company that distributes several intensive phonics systems, including Recipe for Reading.
Hooked on Phonics *www.hop.com*	A complete kit for teaching your child to read using a systematic phonics approach. Kit includes audiotapes and cards for teaching the letter-sound correspondences, a workbook with activities, and books for practicing. Currently sells for around $300.
K12.com	A new on-line school that offers parents and educators an Internet-delivered curriculum that includes phonics and literature programs.
Read, Write, and Type	A software program distributed by the Learning Company for under $200. This program offers the student practice and reinforcement on letter-sound correspondence, as well as instruction in typing.
Saxon Phonics *www.saxonpub.com* 1-800-284-7019	Saxon Publishers has a catalog for home use called Home Study Catalog. Includes systematic phonics (and math) programs.

cont.

Scholastic Interactive Phonics Readers *www.scholastic.com*	Well-designed computer-based instruction on CD-ROM with supplementary decodable books (Phonics Readers).
The Sonday System *www.readabc.com*	A complete kit that includes a video-tape, letter cards, and an instruction guide. Currently sells for around $300.

How do I decide when it's time to have my child tested?

I am very concerned that my daughter, who is seven years old, may be dyslexic. She has been saying things like "the hot is house" when she means it is hot in the house. This type of oral language reversal occurs frequently and she is having trouble remembering letters and sounds. I was diagnosed with dyslexia and attention deficit disorder when I was in first grade in 1970. My daughter's teacher is not taking these concerns seriously. She often says to me "she will develop in her own time" and "you are overly concerned" because she is my first child. I never did learn to read within the school system and only began reading in eleventh grade after my mother found a tutor outside of school. I'm concerned that she is going to fall behind and will never catch up. I don't want to waste any unnecessary time. Should my child be tested?

The parent should act on behalf of this child for several reasons. It is not too early for testing: any seven-year-old can be assessed with a reasonable degree of accuracy. She has a family history of dyslexia and is demonstrating several warning signs of learning disabilities. The difficulty this parent describes is with the most important aspects of beginning reading. The child is also old enough to have had some instruction in reading and is not learning easily. At age seven this child can and should have full psychoeducational, language, and audiological testing. For a child with several risk factors who is demonstrating difficulty, there is no reason to wait until second or third grade. She can and should be tested by the end of first grade.

What is the earliest age you can test a child for dyslexia?

At the end of first grade the school was telling me that my son was a "beginning reader." He didn't seem like a beginning reader to me! He attended kindergarten for two years and had started school with an active IEP for speech and language issues. By the end of first grade he had received private speech one-on-one for three years. His private speech therapist told me to request testing for a learning disability by the school because she felt something was seriously wrong. What should I do?

This parent has described two separate but related concerns—speech delays and dyslexia. Any child older than three or four who is not speaking clearly should be screened at a local school for possible speech and language delays. Children with speech delays often benefit from speech and language therapy during the preschool years because that is the optimal time for learning oral language. In addition, it is well known that children who have speech and language delays in the preschool years are at great risk for reading problems in first grade. In fact, studies show that between 75 and 100 percent of children with preschool language delays have trouble learning to read.

The science of diagnosis and prediction of reading problems has now progressed to the point where a five-year-old can be reliably assessed. The evaluation would focus on such pre-reading skills as knowledge of letter names, letter sounds, rhyming, sound identification, concepts of print, and oral language development. Even though the child is not yet reading, the ability to read is dependent on these skills, and a fairly good judgment about the child's needs can be made. The child should be reassessed before the end of first grade to confirm the initial findings, but there is no reason to wait until the child is actually taught how to read.

Speech and language therapy should include preparatory work on alphabetic and phonological skills. Such intervention can begin without a complete psychoeducational assessment. The parents can help at home by developing the child's oral language, reading books aloud, singing nursery rhyme songs, and playing word games that draw the child's attention to the sounds in words. The child's kindergarten teacher should be using both a classroom screening tool, such as Fox in a Box (see table on assessment tools in Appendix 1), and a program of systematic phonological, language, and early literacy skill development for the classroom.

First graders should be assessed by their teacher every six to eight weeks. The teacher should know how they are progressing in learning letter-sound correspondences, decoding simple words, spelling regular words and some sight words, and comprehending the information in books. Ideally, more intensive help should be available for students who are falling behind. Some teachers take small groups within the classroom to give them extra attention; others have the assistance of tutors who review and bolster the classroom instruction.

If students are struggling after receiving extra help in kindergarten and throughout first grade, they would be good candidates for a complete assessment. With effective intervention programs, referrals for special education services should be reduced significantly. Only those with serious handicaps will need to be in special education classes if classroom instruction is excellent and extra help is provided as soon as children begin to struggle. Special education services can ultimately be more effective if they are reserved for a smaller number of students who need intensive systematic structured teaching of language skills.

How do I select a person to test my child if I suspect dyslexia?

Today we had our IEP [Individualized Education Plan] meeting for our seven-year-old son. The "team" was not able to come to a definite conclusion that our son has a learning disability in reading. They do not feel that extremely poor decoding skills qualifies as a disability under IDEA. We then requested an independent evaluation, which the district has agreed to. Unfortunately, none of the evaluators listed on the Illinois state list of independent evaluators is also listed on the list from the Illinois branch of the International Dyslexia Association. Are these people truly independent? How can I select a good evaluator or find out information about these people on the state's list?

The questions raised by this parent are extremely important but often difficult to answer. One question is how to select a competent evaluator. Probably the most important characteristic of the person whom you select to test your child is his or her understanding of reading and language processes and familiarity with dyslexia research. This understanding underlies the ability to construct the most appropriate battery of standardized tests and observe your child's difficulties in more informal tasks. Psychologists, unfortunately, often have no formal training in these areas, and if they decide to specialize in LD evaluations, they must obtain additional training on their own. Many people are certified to give the Wechsler or the Woodcock-Johnson tests, the most frequently used tests for IQ and achievement, but they may have little ability to interpret them in light of current knowledge about dyslexia or language-based reading disorders. The most common shortcoming of these evaluators is the lack of training in linguistics and reading development. Evaluators who are well qualified often have training in several disciplines, such as linguistics, reading education, and psychology.

Diagnosis involves more than obtaining a set of test scores. Test scores, like X rays or lab tests in medicine, must be viewed as indicators of underlying conditions. One of the arts of diagnosis is careful observation of how a child responds to questions or tasks. Another is the ability to see patterns in all the data, including parent and teacher reports, test scores, and response style. Informal indicators of a problem, such as the manner in which a child goes about spelling words with certain sounds, can be just as important as standardized test scores in formulating a diagnosis. An informed evaluator knows how to analyze the errors on a spelling list, make sense of how a child decodes words, and make astute observations by listening to the way the child constructs sentences both orally and in writing.

Evaluators who really understand reading and language learning difficulties look for a configuration of symptoms across all sources of information.

Common Symptoms of Dyslexia

- Relative difficulty on timed tests of reading, both oral and written, especially on the Gray Oral Reading Test and the Test of Word Reading Efficiency.
- Poor spelling achievement on the Test of Written Spelling, the Wide Range Achievement Test, and the Wechsler Individual Achievement Test in relation to verbal reasoning ability and reading comprehension.
- Relative difficulty on tests of nonsense word reading and

cont.

sound-letter associations, such as the word attack subtests of the Woodcock-Johnson, Woodcock Reading Mastery, and Decoding Skills Tests.

- Low scores on tests of phonological skills such as the Comprehensive Test of Phonological Processing, the Lindamood Auditory Conceptualization Test, and the Rosner Test of Auditory Analysis Skills.

- Relatively low score on Digit Span of the WISC-III or memory for lists of unrelated numbers and words (short-term phonological memory tests).

- Oral vocabulary or verbal reasoning test scores that are higher than specific word reading or spelling ability.

- Inability to spell the sounds in words using a phonetic strategy (FOIES for *fish)* or inability to remember the spellings of irregular but common words such as *of, to, said,* and *does.*

- Difficulty in forming printed or cursive letters; messy-looking handwriting, disorganized written work, and problems with spelling, punctuation, and capitalization.

- Listening comprehension that exceeds reading comprehension.

- Nonlanguage skills that are better developed, including the ability to complete the performance or spatial subtests on the WISC-III (Block Design, Object Assembly, Picture Completion).

It is important to realize that few individuals have all of these symptoms and that none of these symptoms alone determines the diagnosis. It is the preponderance of symptoms and the convergence of symptoms that the evaluator considers in deciding on an appropriate diagnosis. Thus, there are borderline cases about whom evaluators might disagree, especially among people who function well.

The person whom you want to test your child will most likely have doctoral-level training in psychology, educational psychology, reading, or learning disabilities and an established history of providing assessments. It is an advantage if the person works with other professionals whose skills are in other areas, so that several experts meet your child and compare notes and observations.

The parent network is often most helpful in determining who in your area does the best job. If you contact other parents whose children receive special education services at your school, they are often willing to share experiences they have had with various evaluators. The president of an organization for parents of children with special needs is usually well informed. Even if an evaluator comes with excellent recommendations, however, you should consider making an initial appointment to interview that person.

Usually, the school district prefers that a parent work with an evaluator that both have agreed on, and will work with a family to review the evaluator's credentials and operating procedures. A district can be instrumental in getting a new evaluator's name on the state's approved list if you can demonstrate that the person you wish to see is qualified and will not charge an unreasonable fee for the work. You are also free to refuse to work with an evaluator selected by the district if you have a good reason to believe that the person is not qualified. The interview questions and the lists of diagnostic tests in this chapter should provide you with the information you need to negotiate with the district about who will test your child.

Interview Questions to Ask
Before Hiring an Evaluator

- What is your training?
- What licenses do you hold?
- How long have you been evaluating children? How many children do you test in a month?
- Are you familiar with dyslexia as a diagnostic term? What does it mean to you? Do you use this term in your reports? Why or why not?
- What are some of the tests you give to evaluate reading and language problems? (Compare the response to the list of assessments in this chapter.)
- What are some of the informal assessments that you give a child who is having difficulty with reading? (Dictate spelling list, write a paragraph, listen to the child's oral language, etc.)
- Will you be able to refer us to an educational therapist or qualified reading teacher? How do you know the person is qualified to provide instruction?
- Will you meet with us when the testing is done?
- Will you provide a written report as part of the fee? What will be discussed in the report?
- If my child has a reading disability, will you recommend a specific method for teaching him to read? (Structured systematic language approach that uses multisensory techniques [MSL], or one of the programs such as Orton-Gillingham, etc.)
- Are you able to meet with my child's teachers at school, if needed?
- Are you familiar with the Educational Testing Service's requirements to apply for extended time on the SAT test?

Do I have any legal rights to insist that the school test my child?

My daughter has had reading difficulties since kindergarten. She repeated first grade and is currently in second grade. She has made progress over the years, but it has been labored and slow. She is a bright, wonderful little girl who wants so much to read books on her own, but gets frustrated when she can't recall words or sound them out. Her spelling skills are weak as well. I had a parent-teacher conference at the beginning of the school year where I learned from the teacher that my daughter was in the bottom 3 percent of the lowest reading group, despite being one of the oldest in the class. I have learned a lot about dyslexia the past year and have requested that the school test her. The classroom teacher now says that my daughter is performing at grade level given that she received an honor roll report card for the first quarter grading period. I am getting a little nervous about the meeting because I get the feeling that the child study team may deny my daughter eligibility for special education services.

Parents do have legal rights to request that the school test a child who is suspected of having a learning disability. However, the school district has the right to decide which children it will test. Even though schools are required under federal law (the Individuals with Disabilities Education Act) to identify children who are disabled, including learning-disabled, the school is not required to test a child just because the parent has requested it. Parents, however, still have recourse if the school refuses to test a child and the child is subsequently diagnosed as learning-disabled by a private evaluator. In that case, the school district could be asked by a hearing officer to reimburse the family for the cost of testing. Ultimately, school district administrators often lean toward fulfilling parental requests for testing just to save time and expense in the long run. Only in cases where the child is obviously doing very well in school will districts take a strong stand against testing.

Always make your request for testing in writing in a letter to the principal and be sure the letter is dated. In the letter you should specifically say that you are concerned that your child may have a learning disability. According to the law, the school district has sixty days to evaluate the child, and if the child does qualify for services as a student with a learning disability, the district has another thirty days to meet and develop his individualized education plan (IEP).

School administrators have a difficult job to do. They have to balance the needs of all the students in the school, and their budgets are usually underfunded to begin with. If testing is conducted on children who do not need to be tested, there will not be enough money for the ones who do need it. Administrators are constantly making difficult choices about individuals so as to serve the needs of the entire community.

Steps to Request That the School Test Your Child

- Discuss your concerns about your child's difficulties with his teacher.
- Observe your child in his classroom.
- Make notes of your observations about your child's difficulties both in and outside the classroom.
- Keep notes about each conversation you have with the teacher about your concerns.
- After several conversations, ask the teacher to recommend your child for testing.
- Become informed about the warning signs of learning disabilities by reviewing the list of the Coordinated Council for Learning Disabilities so you can cite these concerns in your letter (www.ldonline.org).
- Write a letter to the principal requesting that your child be tested for a learning disability.

How do I find out about my legal rights?

Our son, who is eleven and in sixth grade, seems to have some sort of a processing or attention problem, especially in regard to reading. He is lacking in reading comprehension, as evidenced by his recent score on the Stanford Achievement Test, where he was in the 6th percentile in that area. He managed to get on the honor roll at school last quarter and wants to do well in school. When I requested professional evaluation via the reading teacher on his sixth-grade team, she looked into it and responded that the school is currently "in between" psychologists. His teacher was also told by school personnel that they don't test for dyslexia. What are our rights within the school?

This parent needs to do some research about her child's rights under IDEA. Consult our recommended resources and some of the books about legal rights listed in Appendix 2 as well. Plan to begin attending conferences and researching on your own. Chapter 9 provides more information about your legal rights within IDEA and other laws. Be aware that although we freely use the term "dyslexia" in this book, you may live in a state where the term is nowhere to be found in regulations governing special educational services, and nowhere to be found in the training or professional development of teachers. Part of getting the help your child needs may involve the deliberate use of certain terms such as "reading disability" or "learning disability" rather than "dyslexia."

If the school does the testing, is there anything I can do to assure that it is done properly?

You do not have the right to control how the school does its evaluation. Your job is to evaluate the quality of the testing the school did and advocate for independent testing if the school's results don't seem right to you or do not make sense.

The school will most likely use its own staff psychologist to do the testing. You will probably not have any control over the district's choice of an evaluator. If the district is large enough to have more than one psychologist on staff, then you might want to do some homework and try to influence which one tests your child.

Unfortunately, some districts hire psychologists just out of graduate school in order to save money. The interns do need experience, and this job gives them plenty of experience in testing children. However, inexperienced interns may not have the perspective or academic knowledge needed to make diagnostic judgments and may not be able to make the crucial observations of error patterns or test behavior that an expert would make. In addition, they will often give a minimal test battery for the purpose of comparing ability and achievement scores. The test battery may omit other critical tests (such as phonological processing). Watching how the child goes about solving problems, observing whether he forms his letters from the top down or bottom up, and seeing how he approaches unknown words are all important pieces of information for an evaluator to observe. Again, the assessment should be done by an experienced person with deep knowledge of language, reading, and instruction.

If the school tests my child and I don't agree with the results, what can I do?

You can always have your child tested by someone outside the school and submit the results to the school to include in an IEP meeting. The school must consider the results, but it doesn't necessarily have to agree with your expert. The school rarely pays for this outside evaluation, although many parents consider this money well spent. When a case goes to due process to resolve a disagreement between the parent and the school over the child's diagnosis or services, almost always an independent psychologist is hired by the family.

One parent has her child independently assessed once a year to quantify the child's progress. By submitting this test result to the district, the parent is making certain that her evaluator, an unbiased person, retains control over use of a major testing instrument. The school would be unable to use this same instrument because of guidelines about how frequently the same test can be given to a child. This parent has adopted this strategy to ensure the reliability of test results pertaining to the student's progress in the key area of his IEP.

Is it better to have my child tested privately or allow the school to do the testing?

If the school is willing to do the testing, most parents allow it to do so. You can always have your child tested privately later. Even though there are guidelines that prohibit administration of the same test within a certain amount of time, there are enough alternative tests so that evaluators can find other ways to measure the same areas of functioning.

There are a number of reasons why parents might want to have their child tested privately. Some want confidentiality, and others want to have control over who does the testing. For families who have the financial resources the decision may center on where you believe you will get the best information. It is important to realize, however, that you have to do your homework in choosing an evaluator who is informed about language, reading, and reading disability. Some of the benefits and drawbacks to each approach are shown in the following table:

Analysis of Privately Contracted vs. School Testing from Viewpoint of the Parent

School Testing	Private Testing
QUALITY	
• No control over who does testing.	• Parent selects evaluator.
• No control over environment where testing is done.	• Testing is usually done in quiet environment.
	• Evaluator usually gives a thorough analysis with a full written and verbal report of results.
COST	
• No cost to parent.	• Can be very expensive ($1,200–$2,000).
CONTROL	
• No authority to decide when testing is needed.	• Parent decides when it's time to test.
• No control over when child is pulled from class for testing.	• Privacy: parent has control over whom to release test results to and report to.
• School district is required to keep results in child's permanent file, although there are confidentiality rules.	
AVAILABILITY	
• IDEA specifies that testing must be completed within sixty days.	• Can be difficult to find a qualified evaluator.
	• Evaluator may have a long waiting list.

If you just want reassurance that your child is reading on grade level, hire a private educational therapist or reading specialist to give you an opinion. One advantage of using a private therapist who works with children with reading difficulties is that this person is knowledgeable about the signs of learning disabilities—probably more knowledgeable than many people who work at large, commercial learning centers.

If you are more concerned than curious, then it may be more appropriate to jump directly to having a learning clinic do a specific assessment of language-related skills. You may also jump directly to a full psychoeducational evaluation. Finally, deciding who will do the testing is important because not all evaluators are equally well informed about diagnosing language-related learning problems and other learning disabilities. Here is some final advice on testing:

Advice about Testing

- *Don't go on a fishing expedition.* Know what you are concerned about. Lead the whole process from beginning to end. Develop a specific referral question about your concerns. The more you know about why you want testing, the easier it will be to select the right evaluator and lead him or her toward choosing specialized tests.

- *Select an evaluator who is especially knowledgeable about the learning disability or problem you are concerned about.* Some specialize in attention deficit disorder, while others are more knowledgeable about reading, math, or writing. Interview the evaluator to determine her specialties before hiring her. Ask the same questions of the school district's psychologist that you would ask of an independent expert you are hiring.

- *Keep notes about your observations of what is difficult for your child.* Use these notes in your interview with the evaluator.

- *Before you hire an evaluator, ask what tests will be performed.* Compare what the evaluator says to the list of tests in this chapter. The evaluator should have a strategy for assessing each area on the list.

chapter 6

Seeking a Diagnosis

I am trying to decide whether to have my child tested. Although our health plan will cover testing, I am still reluctant, as it may label my daughter forever more as "LD." I know that the important thing is that she gets help, label or no label. But like it or not, some labels may be detrimental. Her teacher and her tutor suggest that I do it anyway, "just so we'll know," and also that she'll know and have a reason for the way that she learns. By the way, I asked her teacher this morning if the school would do the testing and she hesitated, then told me confidentially that they are told to tell parents that dyslexia is a "medical diagnosis" and that testing is not something they will do.

Unfortunately, this parent is not the only parent to have had this kind of experience. The teacher delivered two messages to the parent. First, the teacher discouraged the parent from asking for testing, although testing is a legal right under special education law. The teacher's second message was that even if the school tests the child, it will not use the term "dyslexia" and will not acknowledge the legitimacy of the concept.

Your child may well fit the criteria for dyslexia even though the school has never used the term. If your child exhibits many of the characteristics, you may wish to ask a specialist to review the school's report to get another opinion and more clarification. Again, your goal is to determine if the school is using the best approach to teach your child, and to determine if she is making good progress. Experts who are familiar with and who use the term "dyslexia" are most often able to make that judgment.

This mother is also concerned about the possible negative consequences of her child being identified as learning-disabled—a concern that is shared by many parents. There is so much misinformation about learning disabilities and there are so many problems with the education system that is supposed to serve this group that worries about negative consequences of labeling are legitimate.

Other parents have found that the identification of the problem provides relief, information, and access to resources. A diagnosis can validate observations, and it provides a direction for a parent's research, including guidance about what kinds of help are likely to be beneficial. Some children are relieved to have a clear diagnosis and to learn that the problem they are having is not their fault.

In this chapter we are going to explore some reasons why obtaining a diagnosis is useful, as well as some situations in which a diagnosis may be unnecessary. We are also going to discuss why written reports from evaluators often do not specify a diagnosis of dyslexia, even when the child has many of the characteristics.

When do we need a diagnosis of the specific learning disability?

If your child is school-aged and is not getting the help she needs from the school, then unfortunately you may have to get a diagnosis and go through a protracted eligibility process in order to use legal leverage to access special services. Unless the school agrees to give responsibility to an outside evaluator, the school will conduct the testing to determine the child's eligibility for services.

Parents who opt to have their child tested privately need to anticipate the need for a formal diagnosis. Licensed psychologists, physicians, and doctoral-level specialists in learning disabilities with a multidisciplinary background are the professionals most likely to conclude their reports with a formal diagnosis of a disorder. The diagnostic handbook of the American Psychological Association (DSM-IV) is the source of the categories and terms that are used. School psychologists, learning specialists, and nondoctoral psychometricians usually do not use formal diagnostic terminology because (a) they are not licensed to do so and (b) special education law does not require it. In the preceding chapter we suggested that there are different levels of assessment and that you do not always need to seek full testing immediately, depending upon what you are trying to learn. Yet it is important to know that the only type of testing that will result in a specific diagnosis is full psychoeducational evaluation in which a doctoral-level specialist participates.

We support and encourage the practice of screening young children and giving them direct instruction before they are referred for testing. If your school has a program to identify children who are at risk for reading difficulty in mid-kindergarten and the school delivers intervention immediately, waiting for an assessment is a good idea. If an appropriate type of intervention is offered immediately by an informed and well-trained teacher and at an appropriate level of intensity, your child may get a good start in reading before she ever falls far behind. If the program has continuity, she will go right into a first-grade program that uses best practices in instruction. For many children who have mild characteristics of dyslexia—especially weak phonological skills—this early intervention may be all they need. Under these conditions, referrals to special education should be reduced.[1]

If I'm going to provide help privately, is it better to spend my money on testing or tutoring?

A reading tutor I have hired for my daughter firmly believes in the Orton-Gillingham method and they started together yesterday. My question is, should I still have her tested for dyslexia? She fits all the descriptions I've read about: late talker, has trouble finding the right word, still says "aminal" and other syllable mix-ups, etc. But what good will having a formal diagnosis do? As I said, I have hired a reading tutor for her, we always read aloud together by taking turns, and we go to the library. If we're already taking the steps to help her with her dyslexia, what good will a diagnosis do?

This parent has obviously already done a great deal of research, as she not only knows that her seven-year-old daughter is exhibiting some of the classic characteristics of dyslexia, but more important she has hired a language therapist ("tutor") trained in the Orton-Gillingham approach. It is very likely that if her daughter is tested and diagnosed with dyslexia, this kind of tutoring is exactly what an informed evaluator would recommend. So in this family's case, there is clearly no urgency for testing, especially because they are getting an early start with a child who is only seven.

When parents ask whether it is better to spend money on testing or tutoring, there is no clear answer. It depends on whether the child has multiple difficulties, how much the parent knows about the child's problems, and what kind of expertise the tutor can offer. There is no harm in trying tutoring first to see how the child responds to instruction and to see what the teacher discovers from instruction itself. The key is to hire a very skilled and trained teacher who will use a structured systematic language approach. Reading skills are taught in a systematic and explicit way using techniques that engage several senses simultaneously. If your child makes demonstrable progress that enables her to catch up to grade level within six to twelve months of tutoring, then you may not need testing. You can always test later if she doesn't make enough progress or if the tutor feels there are other difficulties beyond the phonological deficit that are impeding her ability to learn to read.

For parents who are just learning about learning disabilities and effective approaches for teaching children to read, testing may be an important way to get information and guidance. A detailed written report also helps the tutor understand the child's instructional needs. Some tutors understand testing well and develop a rationale for instruction from looking at the child's scores. Testing can also provide you with information in a manner (charts, graphs, scores) that helps you explain your child's difficulties to her and to her teachers.

Sometimes testing reveals a problem in another area that might have been undetected. For example, the child may process information slowly on a rapid naming test or word recognition test. Although the child's immediate problem may seem to be sound-letter association, an accompanying deficit in speed of word retrieval complicates her efforts to learn to read. Similarly, problems in nonverbal, visual-spatial skills may affect reading comprehension later on, because she might have difficulty in understanding part to whole relationships, cause and effect logic, or classification.

If you decide to begin tutoring immediately and defer testing, consider that issues you are putting aside may very well crop up later in the child's school career. Many children who receive early and effective intervention for phonemic awareness and decoding can become successful readers. However, most of the time their problems and your need to intervene with them will not be over at this point. Often students have difficulty with other language-related skills, including spelling, written expression, and learning a foreign language. A child with dyslexia typically has even more difficulty with spelling and writing than she does with reading. Those are the most complex language skills to master. Knowing how to spell a word requires an even more developed sense of letter-sound associations than being able to recognize a word in print. The student's writing is often immature, poorly expressed, brief, and filled with errors. She may choose to write only simple words that she can spell, words that are not nearly as descriptive as she chooses in her oral expression, and she may find the whole effort of writing frustrating and tiring.

If you decide to delay testing and provide your child with expert multisensory structural language tutoring, you should be aware that if you need a diagnosis later, you will need to use a well-informed evaluator. It is more difficult to diagnose dyslexia in a student whose reading is at grade level. The evaluator must have broad knowledge of the many dimensions of dyslexia in order to recognize the symptoms in speech, spelling, writing, study skills, and speed of reading.

If my child is tested by the school, will we get a specific diagnosis?

For a number of reasons the school-based evaluation team may not use the term "dyslexia" or other specific learning disability terms recognized by researchers. If you give permission for your child to be tested (the school will ask for written permission to test your child), the school's testing may not bring a specific diagnosis or the clarity and insights into your child's learning problems that you are so desperately seeking. Here's the way one parent sees it:

We have been round and round with our eleven-year-old daughter's teaching staff, principal, and district representatives in order to try and define what our daughter's disabilities are. The school district seems to think that nothing further should be done. She has poor spelling, poor reading, and number confusion, yet is otherwise a bright and happy girl who is very creative and able to solve real-world problems that do not require reading. She was tested in third grade by her school, and as a result, it was determined that she requires some assistance and more time in order to process information and has poor reading and comprehension scores. Other than that, there was no direction. She is becoming more and more frustrated with school. We are extremely frustrated at the school's reluctance to help us locate solutions to her problems.

In this case the assessment conducted by the school evaluation team resulted in the child being eligible for some special education services, but the parents feel the educational program lacks a clear rationale. They must still seek expert advice to resolve these frustrations.

Many school-based evaluations include a lot of testing that is never pulled together into a coherent statement of disability and instructional need. The exercise can be quite meaningless if those who are doing the testing lack expertise in dyslexia or other disorders. An expert evaluator will try to pinpoint the exact areas of difficulty and interpret their meaning, but they, too, may not write in a way that communicates. Sophisticated diagnosticians may work with concepts or tests unfamiliar to school personnel, such as brain-behavior phenomena, that have little meaning to the team that must instruct. Only the very best (and hard-to-find) evaluators successfully bridge the gap between the insights to be gained from assessment and interpretations that are useful to teachers.

The most critical issue with regard to testing is whether the exercise leads to an understanding of and implementation of effective instruction. Even though the child's Individualized Education Plan (IEP) is supposed to be based on the child's unique needs, too often schools provide the methodology that they have rather than what is actually needed for the child to make the most progress. For example, if the school uses Direct Instruction (Reading Mastery) or is heavily invested in Reading Recovery and that is all it knows and can do, a private evaluator's recommendations may go unheeded if he or she includes a different approach that requires special training or materials. Very few special education or reading teachers in public school settings have the experience, expertise, and time to deliver what evaluators recommend. In fact, many special education teachers have too many children, too little training, too little support, and too few resources to be all things to all students.

As a parent you cannot prescribe the testing or the teaching methodology, but you can insist on progress. You need to make sure that the IEP goals are specific enough so that if your child fails to make progress with the school's approach, you can demand that something else be done. You may need to argue for another teaching methodology or the provision of outside services (at the school's expense).

The mother quoted above needs to first document her views in writing and then ask the school for an independent evaluator to test her child. If she decides to hire her own independent evaluator, it is still wise to document her intention in writing before hiring the outside expert in case she brings a suit to get reimbursed by the school district for the expense.

Families also need to know that even the best evaluators do not always have the explanations and answers they are seeking. Although we understand the nature of language-based reading and spelling difficulty much better than we understand some other kinds of learning disorders, the state of learning disability assessment is quite primitive compared to some other branches of science. Often the best we can do is prescribe research-validated approaches to instruction that are usually effective and helpful. We do not always know if they will work, for whom they will work best, or why they work. Only a very sophisticated evaluator will be aware of the limits, as well as the explanatory power, of the test results.

Are there any other benefits from having a diagnosis?

Navigating toward insight and solutions is inherently difficult, but the journey through choices may seem even foggier without a good assessment or diagnosis. At least if your child's report states a diagnosis such as "developmental reading disability (dyslexia)," then you can gain access to resources such as the International Dyslexia Association.

You may be able to counsel your own child much more effectively if her problem has a specific name. Many students who struggle do not understand their own learning challenges, and labeling those challenges appropriately can help children embrace the help that is offered.

Why do some evaluators not use the word "dyslexia" in the written report?

I have a child who is eight years old and in second grade. She is really struggling in school and I have suspected dyslexia for some time now. She is almost a year behind in reading. I recently had a full evaluation done privately, and the psychologist told me after testing that she was very confident that my daughter was dyslexic and had a "language processing disorder." However, when I got the written report, neither word was anywhere in there. The conclusion was listed as a "reading disorder." Is a reading disorder dyslexia? Why didn't the report say the diagnosis was dyslexia?

Many evaluators do not use the word "dyslexia" in a written report for a variety of complex reasons. The evaluator in this case may not feel informed enough to use the term in her report, or she may be conforming to conventions of her profession. She may also be trying to select terms she feels will be best understood by others who read the report. Psychologists tend to use the term "specific developmental reading disorder," again because the professional handbook for psychologists uses that term. Experts from other disciplines may use different terminology.

Not all psychologists are experts in all learning disabilities. Some psychologists are good at diagnosing dyslexia, others at ADD and ADHD, and others at nonverbal learning disabilities. If you suspect your child is dyslexic, then it is critical to choose an evaluator who is an expert at diagnosing dyslexia. If you suspect some other kind of learning problem, try to find someone with expertise in that area.

State regulations for diagnosing a learning disability may also require terms such as "auditory" or "visual processing deficit." These are outmoded terms, no longer used by researchers because they are vague, easy to misinterpret, and unrelated to any intervention or treatment that works.

I (Susan) have had firsthand experience with the consequences of *not* using the term "dyslexia." Through all the research I did and my involvement as a volunteer with the International Dyslexia Association, I knew that my son's difficulties matched a great number of the warning signs of dyslexia. However, the diagnostic report we received from a private evaluator indicated only that he had a learning disability and an auditory processing deficit. Even though I was fairly certain that my son was dyslexic, I was reluctant to tell him he was dyslexic without a professional opinion to back me up. I had been providing him with exactly the kind of help a dyslexic child benefits from, and it was working. Yet I needed confirmation from an expert. I eventually flew him to California, where Pat Lindamood of Lindamood-Bell Learning Processes evaluated him. Louisa Moats also reviewed our son's full testing file, examined his written work and a spelling assessment she gave him, and she confirmed his dyslexia. That enabled me to feel confident that "dyslexia" was the right term for his difficulties. Until then, I was tentative and expended too much energy wondering what was going on.

Why do some people believe that the term "learning difference" is preferable to "learning disability"?

In spite of the fact that some parents often benefit from receiving a diagnosis for their child, some well-respected experts prefer the term "learning difference" because they view it as less damaging to the child's self-esteem. Whether you want to soft-pedal the label or not depends on your goals and the severity of the child's difficulty.

Parents should try to communicate a positive view of their child's learning disability to the child, other family members, and the child's educators. You must be convinced that your child *can* do well in school with the proper instruction and accommodations and that despite school struggles, your child will ultimately succeed in life. Children can survive a great deal of stress if they know that the most important adults in their life believe in them. Keeping a positive attitude in the beginning of the discovery process can be very hard, especially when the person who evaluates your child gives you a dim view of the child's prospects for succeeding in school, college, or life.

Our family (Susan's) experienced such pessimism. A psychologist told us that our son's learning disability was mild to moderate and that we should modify our expectations for him. We were very disappointed, but we believed that our son was much more capable than the psychologist had judged. As we later discovered, the psychologist had underestimated our son's tremendous strengths and took an unnecessarily dim view of his prospects. He was also misinformed about dyslexia and the power of early and appropriate intervention.

We decided we would do everything possible and provide our child with the best services, which we determined were available privately and not through our local public school. It paid off. Our son is successful because he received early and effective intervention for his reading difficulty. By the month before he started second grade, he was receiving private tutoring by an expert tutor who used the Orton-Gillingham approach, and the help was not only effective but also intensive enough that he caught up to grade level in reading by mid-second grade. He also received additional private tutoring from time to time, including five weeks at a Lindamood-Bell clinic one summer.

Our son is now in eighth grade, and he receives almost no special accommodations for his dyslexia. He attends a private school where the academic rigor is high, and he is getting mostly As with a few Bs. He reads the same books as every other child in the class and does all the same work as everyone else. He receives private tutoring to help him learn to write better and has also received some tutoring in algebra. Over the past couple of years we invested a lot of time to help him learn good study habits and strong study skills. Sometimes he gets frustrated at the difficulty of some subjects, but he is completely optimistic about his future.

Children with learning disabilities need to know about the importance of their study and organizational skills. They may need to work harder, or work in different ways, in order to be as successful as their peers. It is important to help a child with a learning disability learn techniques such as outlining chapters, composing outlines before beginning to write a paper, organizing sentences within a paragraph, and especially tips and techniques for editing their work. In learning a foreign language, often children with dyslexia incorporate some of the same techniques they used for learning to read. They can make color-coded flash cards to help them remember masculine and feminine nouns.

Parents may enjoy reading, viewing, or hearing stories of successful people who have overcome their challenges. The resource list in Appendix 2 includes some biographical stories. Regardless of what term you use, it *is* important for a student with a learning disability to understand that she *can* learn and to become aware of *how* she learns best. The parents and teachers in a child's life need to help the student understand herself, not feel defeated, and focus energy on helping her learn how to learn. A positive attitude can make a big difference.

When should I tell my child about her learning disability?

Most parents find that by the time they have their child tested she is already aware that something is not right. Unfortunately, most children believe that the reason they are having trouble learning is that they are stupid. Usually, their fears are worse than the truth. Most children are aware of their difficulties and report feeling relieved to have a reason and explanation, as well as a plan of action. Sometimes the child is more comfortable with the term than her parents, because having a learning disability is a lot better than just feeling stupid. Here's what one mother wrote to us on our website:

My son's self-esteem improved so much once we had a diagnosis of dyslexia and could "name" what was going on with him. One day when he was in seventh grade and we were driving home from tutoring, he actually said, "Mom, this is the best year of my life. I'm finally getting my dyslexia fixed." I had to pull off the highway to cry. Knowing what the problem was really helped the entire family. My husband came home from the library with books on dyslexia and became empowered through learning about it. My older son began to understand what was happening in our family and burst into tears one day, stating, "I lost my mother the day my brother caught dyslexia." That was a huge wake-up call for me. I had no idea he was affected so much. I am thankful that he finally had the words to use to tell me what it was like for him and we began to talk about it.

Parents need to think about how they will discuss the evaluation results with their child. When our son (Susan's) was first diagnosed with a learning disability at the end of first grade, we decided to tell him that he needed to be taught to read using a different approach. We told him that we had hired a private tutor and he would be going to her office twice a week for help with his reading. Since he already knew that he couldn't read as well as his peers, he was anxious for help and this made sense to him. Shortly after he started going to his tutor, he knew that her approach was working, and he was relieved that finally he was learning to read.

We chose not to use the term "learning disability" with him in first grade because we couldn't understand the diagnosis of "auditory processing deficit" that was in the written report we had received from the evaluator who tested him. It was something we didn't understand ourselves, and therefore we didn't want to try to explain it to our son. We decided to keep researching and reading until we understood his learning disability. When he was in fifth grade, we confirmed through more testing that he is dyslexic, and then we explained it to him immediately. He is now comfortable telling teachers and peers that he is dyslexic, and he understands why certain tasks are harder for him than they might be for his peers. He needs to know this to be able to advocate for himself.

In considering whether to discuss your child's diagnosis with her, this story may help with the decision:

Last year my husband, at age thirty-four, was losing self-confidence and self-esteem due to difficulties in reading and spelling. My husband is in sales and loves sales. However, when he is taking an order, he is embarrassed by his poor spelling. He went to a Sylvan Learning Center for a reading program for five months. The instructor said he may be dyslexic, but they don't specialize in that. When we talked with his parents about it, they said that he was diagnosed with dyslexia in grade school and had a special tutor for a while in third or fourth grade. Then his parents thought the problem went away. My husband and I were very shocked and surprised to hear this.

chapter 7

How to Recognize Effective Reading Instruction

I have been a school psychologist in the school district of a major U.S. city for the past ten years, and your comments about the need to better educate school personnel ring especially true. I don't need to tell you that, so far as I know, most if not all school psychology training programs don't require any formal instruction in reading or remedial reading. The problem in many schools is the lack of instructional staff trained in the necessary techniques of effective remediation. As you know, even the LD teachers in many schools aren't skilled in the techniques you describe in your book *Straight Talk About Reading.* In addition, LD teachers have been found not to typically individualize instruction for their students. But if anything comes through in your book, it is the need to do so. I think many parents have been led to believe by their public schools that once their child has been found "learning-disabled," all will be well. I wish more attention could be called to the fact that most LD teachers teach to the "mean" of the students in their class at any given point in time and that "individualized instruction" promised by schools is very seldom supplied!

The frank statements of this school psychologist are, in our experience, well founded. He shares our concerns that teachers and psychologists are not well trained to understand language-based learning disorders and dyslexia. Research always takes at least fifteen years to filter into the awareness and practices of the frontline educator, but in this case the translation of research seems especially slow. Children in special education often do not receive the individualized instruction that they are entitled to under the law because either there is no expertise to support it or the specialist is serving too many children. Furthermore, many problems children experience become more serious than they should be because the classroom reading and writing instruction has not been effective.

Once a reading problem has been diagnosed, the next decision a parent must make is what type of reading remediation should be done and who can provide it. If your child will receive help at school, regardless of whether that help will be in the regular classroom, from a reading teacher, or from a special education teacher, you need to be sure a research-supported approach is being used. For parents with sufficient financial resources, the decision of whether to accept services through the school or obtain them privately depends on the quality and type of instruction available in each setting. To help you decide on a plan of action, we suggest that you ask a number of specific questions.

The following resources will be provided in this chapter:

- Information on classroom reading instruction and what it should include.

- Descriptions of what effective reading instruction looks like.
- A list of recommended approaches for a child who is struggling with reading.
- Information about professional development for your child's teacher.

What would a well-designed classroom instructional program include?

The findings of the National Reading Panel pertain to classroom instruction—not to instruction specially designed for students with learning disabilities, as the panel elected not to review the research literature on learning disabilities. It is even more striking, then, that their recommendations were so consistent with the preferred methods that have been advocated by specialists in the remediation of reading difficulties and dyslexia. The panel concluded that there is strong support for the following instructional practices:

- Direct teaching of phonemic awareness, to include phoneme blending and segmentation, so that students become able to identify and recall the speech sounds that are represented by letters.
- Systematic, direct teaching of phonics and the use of sounding-out strategies to read unknown words.
- The use of decodable texts so that children can practice what they have been taught.
- The deliberate development of reading fluency.
- Daily reading of text that is at the right level.
- Vocabulary instruction before, during, and after reading

that emphasizes both definitions and the use of words in context.

- Direct teaching of comprehension through a number of strategies, such as making summaries, diagrams, visual images, and written responses to text.
- Incentives for wide reading of a variety of worthwhile books.

Parents can and should ask what approach the school has adopted. If the school's program lacks some of these components, it may be contributing to the problems of many children. Only the best teachers can create complete and effective reading programs by piecing together all these components. Using good children's books alone is not sufficient for teaching reading. Instructional programs do make a difference in the achievement of children in a classroom, and teachers should not be left to invent them on their own.

No other discipline governed by a professional licensing process puts people through a training course and then turns them loose to do whatever they want. Presumably, the purpose of regulating teacher licensing is to ensure that teachers know the best practices of their profession and can deliver them. What if your local electrician got certified at a master's level and then wired your house any way he wanted to? What if your pharmacist decided to experiment with drug combinations she preferred over the ones that had been approved by the FDA? Yet with teaching, we expect almost nothing in the way of common knowledge and proven practices, even though there is evidence to support specific programs and practices over others.

How can I tell if my child's teacher is teaching reading using methods supported by research?

You've just learned that the National Reading Panel report outlines what the components of effective early reading instruction should be. How can you recognize if your child's teacher uses these "best practices" to teach reading? In order for you to be able to judge classroom practices, we offer a portrait of a teacher using best practices. We'll start with kindergarten and then move to first grade.

DAY IN AN IMAGINARY KINDERGARTEN CLASSROOM

Imagine that you are a visitor to a kindergarten classroom in early December. After the students have arrived in the morning and had some time to play in one of the play areas, the teacher, Mrs. P., invites the children to come over to the rug and sit down in front of her. She begins with a traditional morning meeting, taking attendance, giving messages, checking the calendar, and reviewing the schedule for the day. Following this she begins the language and reading session. She starts by reading a poem from a large copy of a book that she placed on the tray of an easel so that all the students could see it. Before she reads the poem to the children Mrs. P. facilitates a discussion about the title, the topic of the poem, the author and illustrator, and background information the children might bring to understanding the words and subjects in the poem. She models how a book is read by pointing to the words as she reads them so that it is clear she is reading from left to right. She moves her finger from the bottom right of a left-hand page to the top left corner of the facing page as she reads. Then the children play a game of replacing the last word in selected rhyming lines of the poem. They create verses that are funny with new, silly, rhyming words. It is clear that all but one or two children not only understand the concept of rhyming words but can join in and think of rhyming words that make the verses even funnier.

For the next activity the children stay seated on the rug. This time they are going to play a game in which the teacher uses a puppet to play an oral word game. The puppet says the sound of /p/ and the teacher says the rest of a word that begins with that sound. Then the teacher has the children clap as they blend the whole word together and say the whole word out loud. For example, the puppet says /p/ and the teacher says /uppet/. Mrs. P. says, "What's the word?" and the children respond "puppet." This activity continues for about ten minutes, with the teacher helping the children blend words.

After the blending game, the children are asked to return to their seats. Mrs. P. reviews a letter sound that was introduced earlier in the week. The children listen to an audiotape with a fun song for this week's letter. The letter this week is *Pp,* and after saying and feeling the position of their mouth when they say /p/, the children agree that /p/ is a short, quiet sound made with their lips. Mrs. P. passes out two cards to each child, one with the letter *P* and another with the letter *S.* The letter *S* was introduced a previous week. Mrs. P. has a list of words that begin with one of these two letters. As she reads each word, the children are asked to hold up the card with the letter of the beginning sound. After practicing with about fifteen words it is clear that all the students can tell the difference in the two beginning sounds and associate the correct letter with the beginning sound in the word.

For the final activity of this lesson the teacher demonstrates on the chalkboard how to write the letter *P*. She has the children practice writing the letters by writing them in the air, moving their arm and repeating a chant about how to make capital letter *P*. The children chant, "Start at the top, go down. Go back up to the top again and go around to the middle and stop." Next the children arrange themselves in four lines at the chalkboard. The teacher writes a correct version of the letter on the chalkboard. Each child picks out a different-colored chalk, and when it's his turn, he tries to trace the teacher's *P* as closely as possible.

The children then return to their desks and take out a small whiteboard and marker. They practice writing *P*s on their whiteboards while the teacher circulates to monitor their work. She stops and guides several students by reminding them to say the chant under their breath as they form their letters. Then the children work in individualized workbooks to circle the pictures that begin with the /p/ sound, and write some more *P*s on the lines in their books.

"Workshop" time is next. Students go to one of several stations to manipulate plastic or wooden letter sets, explore shapes and puzzles, browse books, or work with hands-on math materials.

———

In this example of the imaginary kindergarten classroom, all of the activity has occurred in about forty-five to sixty minutes. You will notice that the instruction is fun, gamelike, and varied.

Yet you will also recognize that several activities are developing the students' phonological awareness. Sounds are being recognized, described, discriminated from others, separated out from spoken words, and blended into spoken words. The instruction builds step by step on concepts that have already been taught. The activities will lead up to more demanding games requiring full separation of the speech sounds in words and the use of letters to spell the sounds in simple words. Learning is purposeful, fun, hands-on, and teacher-directed. Children also learn to take turns, listen to others, and follow directions, within the context of an educationally sound activity.

Many teachers use a big-book format to read a story aloud while they help children follow the print and begin to recognize words. Big-book reading is very important for developing concepts about print and the way books are written, handled, and read. They do not, however, replace the systematic, direct teaching about sounds and letters that most children need. In this example the kindergarten teacher was pointing to the words as she read them aloud to teach children the concepts of print.

Concepts of Print That Can Be Demonstrated with a Big Book

- That each page is read from left to right.
- Where to begin reading on the next page.
- That text is read, not the pictures.
- That longer-sounding words usually have more letters.
- That words are separated in print by a blank space.

If big-book reading is used to *replace* direct teaching of sound-letter correspondence or *instead of* direct teaching of sounds and letters in an organized way, it is being misused. As an engaging, shared reading experience that results in discussion and language stimulation, however, big-book reading is desirable.

The letter-of-the-week activity in our imaginary classroom is also quite different from another version of the letter-of-the-week activity that we often see in kindergarten classrooms. On a designated day such as Wednesday each child shows an object he has brought from home that starts with the letter of the week and tells a little bit about the object. Although it might be fun to go around the circle and share, this activity stops far short of explicit phonemic awareness instruction. Just looking at objects whose names begin with the same consonant letter, as in the show-and-tell letter-of-the-week example, does not get the job done. First of all, there are letters that do not stand for the same sound every time, such as *C* (*cat, cereal, cheese*), and there are sounds that are spelled with more than one letter (/sh/, /th/, /wh/, /ch/, /ng/). In addition, finding objects that begin with a particular letter is a very indirect and implicit way of discussing the similar sound of the objects, if indeed the beginning sound is the same. Children might sit through the activity without ever getting the idea that a word is made up of single speech sounds. Some children in that circle may not be paying attention to the fact that all those objects have the same initial sound. Explicit teaching requires the teacher to do something more than show and tell. Is a skill being explicitly modeled by the teacher, taught, and then practiced? Does it make sense to teach that skill at that time?

The kindergarten classroom we have profiled uses the time

wisely to do explicit training in skills including phonemic awareness, letter recognition, expanding sentences, and understanding how books are read. Some sample phonemic awareness activities that you would see in a kindergarten or early-first-grade classroom are shown in the following table, in approximately their order of difficulty.

Examples of Phonemic Awareness Activities for Kindergarten or Early-First-Grade Instruction

Rhyming sentences	Ask the children to fill in the missing rhyming word: A rat is sitting on a _____ (mat). A moose is talking to a _____ (goose). A pig is wearing something on his head called a _____ (wig).
Clapping syllables	The children sit in a circle and clap the number of syllables in each child's name as you go around the circle.
Letter-sound match	Label several boxes with a picture to indicate the beginning sound (like a cat for the /c/ sound). Then give children objects that can be sorted into the boxes by initial consonant sound.
Sound counters	Have children use counters (pennies, blocks, plastic objects) to say the sounds in a word and move a counter, one sound at a time, to indicate distinct sounds.

cont.

	Begin with easy words with only two or three phonemes and gradually use words with more phonemes. These activities are known by educators as Elkonin Boxes or Say It and Move It.
Blending words	Pronounce words in parts and ask the child to say the word that these parts make when blended together. A puppet can be used to pronounce one part of the word while the teacher pronounces the other part. For example, say /l/ and then "ake" and wait for the children to say "lake." It is easier for children to blend a word by syllables or by two parts (st + ake) than it is to blend each individual sound (/s/ + /t/ + /ae/ + /k/).
Deleting initial sounds	Ask the students to listen as you say a word and have them repeat the word after you. Then ask them to say the word without the beginning sound. Say "cake" without the /k/ sound ("ake").
Deleting final sounds	Ask the students to listen as you say a word and have them repeat the word after you. Then ask them to say the word without the final sound. Say "meat" without the /t/ sound ("me").
Color counters	This is a variation of the "sound counters" game above. The only difference is that

cont.

	you ask the child to use the same-colored counter if the same sound is repeated in a word. You can use nonsense words, too. If the word is *pap*, then the first and third counter should be the same color, and a different color from the middle counter.
Sound deletion	Say "stake." Say it again, but don't say /s/. (More advanced: say it again, but don't say /t/.)

DAY IN AN IMAGINARY FIRST-GRADE CLASSROOM

Now let's visualize a first-grade classroom where the teacher is using a systematic and structured phonics approach. Let's say it is January of first grade, and as we look around the room we see sound-spelling cards displayed prominently above the chalkboard. These cards are designed to teach sound aware-ness and the letter or letter combinations that spell a given sound. They include a picture of a key word containing the sound, along with one or more spellings for the sound *(shark = /sh/, sh; ape = /ā/, a, a_e, ai, ay)*. The students are seated at their desks and the teacher, Mrs. G., is at the chalkboard to begin the two-and-a-half-hour morning language arts in-struction by writing some words and asking the children to sound them out together. She begins with *ship, shin, shine, shack, shake, shape,* and *shrimp.* Each time a word is read, Mrs. G. cues the children by pointing to a sound-spelling unit and saying "sound," waiting for the children to give her the sound, and then moving to the next letter or letter group and saying "sound" again. The sounds are gradually blended together as she scoops her hand under letter sequences and says "blend." The children are obviously familiar with this technique because of how crisply they can give the teacher the sounds. This blending exercise is practiced every day; it builds mastery of sounding out an unknown word.[1]

Next Mrs. G. writes the word *sad* on the board. She asks for a volunteer to tell her how to spell *mad.* A small girl anxiously raises her hand and offers a spelling. Mrs. G. writes the word on the board and asks if everyone in the class agrees with that spelling. They do. Then the class works on the words *mane* and *man.* "What's the difference between these two words?" Mrs. G. asks. One child is called upon, and he explains that when you add an *e* to the end of the word, it reaches back over the consonant and changes the sound that the vowel makes. After writing a list of seven words in which only one sound has changed from one word to the next *(kit, kite, site, side, hide, ride, rid),* Mrs. G. asks for a volunteer to read the whole list. Several sentences with the words are also read: "Hide the kite by this side of the shack."

Leaving the two lists created so far, Mrs. G. starts with another word, *age.* After the whole class blends *age* (/ā/, /j/), the teacher writes *cage* below it so that students can compare the two words letter by letter. Mrs. G. says, "If you know the word *age,* then you should know this word [pointing to *cage*]. Who wants to read it?" A boy near the front raises his hand instantly and blends the sounds /k/, /ā/, and /j/. This work at the board takes fifteen to twenty minutes.

Next the teacher asks the students to sit in a circle on the floor because she has a new game for them to play. She explains the rules. A child selects a card from a basket, reads the word, and shows the word to all the students. If it is read correctly, he gives the card to the teacher. Then he walks around the circle behind his classmates and selects a student to pick another word out of the basket. This game continues until all the words have been read correctly. The children love the suspense of who will be picked to choose a word next, and they enjoy helping to decide if the word has been read correctly.

After finishing this tisket-a-tasket game, the children return to their desks. Mrs. G. writes nine words on the board arranged three across and three down. She then says a word and asks for a student to come to the board and point to the word she has said. If the student correctly selects the word, he gets to erase it from the board. After the first set of nine words has been erased, Mrs. G. repeats this activity with another set of nine words. All the words have a common sound-spelling pattern that the students have been previously taught and are now practicing. Today they are working on recognizing words that have the *dge* and *ge* spellings, so *rage* and *dodge* are two of the words on the board at the same time.

The children have already learned all the consonant sounds and all the short and long vowel sounds. The next activity is a game to review the long and short vowel sounds. The teacher asks who would like to be first. A girl starts by rolling a die and announces that she got "long." Then she picks a vowel card from a bucket and informs her classmates that it is an *e.* Now she needs to think of a word that has a long /e/ vowel sound. She pulls on her pigtail for a moment and then beams as she says "eat." Mrs. G. says "Great" and writes *eat* on the board under the column for *Long E.* The game continues until all the children have had a chance to add a word to the vowel chart they created, and they read all the words together aloud. There are many spellings for the long /e/ sound, so the teacher takes words to spell that have an *ee* or *ea* pattern only (*feet, cheat, sheep, please*).

Now Mrs. G. passes out folders containing letter cards in plastic pockets used to store trading cards. She asks each child to find and remove seven letters from his pocket folder—*b, e, g, h, n, t,* and *w.* She then asks which letter is the vowel. The children answer together "e." "So all our words today are going to have an *e* because we have to have a vowel, right?" Mrs. G. says. Then she tells the children that she wants them to spell the words by arranging some of the seven cards. The first word is *hen.* The teacher wanders around the room helping a few children who are not sure which letters to use. Then she continues with the next word, which is *bent,* followed by *when* and *went.* They can also spell the words *he, be,* and *we,* which are in a family of odd words that use only the one letter for the long vowel. The children work on seven or eight words and then stop.

Next the class reads a decodable book—one where the words can be read with what has been previously taught—that is part of the published reading program they are using. The children work in small groups of four to read today's story, which includes many words with this week's new sound. Because the words in these small storybooks are ones that the children can sound out, the teacher doesn't need to coach many children. Each child reads a page aloud to the others in his group. The students will take home a copy of today's story to read to their parents for extra practice and to keep parents involved in their child's reading progress. After all the groups have read the story, the children assemble on a rug to discuss it. This discussion enables the teacher to elaborate concepts, define words, help children retell the story, sequence the events, and draw inferences.

The final activity is independent work time. The children check the chart and proceed to one of four stations in the room. There is a writing station where children are working on writing a page in their journals about an experience at the beach. You can see children checking the sound cards and the word wall for help with spelling as they write. Another group of children is listening to stories on audiotapes with headphones while following along with copies of a book. A third group is quietly playing a board game involving words that have a common spelling pattern. And the last group is gathered around the teacher's desk reading aloud to Mrs. G. while she offers correction as needed, a practice that supports the development of fluency. The children are engaged and quietly participating in these activities for about twenty minutes. Mrs. G. gives a five-minute warning, and after putting their materials away, the children stream out of the classroom door for recess.

Later in the day, other reading or writing activities may occur, such as read-aloud and discussion from a well-chosen book; class letter-writing or bookmaking; or a library search for books about a topic of interest. Although so much time has been devoted to reading, spelling, and writing, there is still time for a thorough math lesson and a science activity. The priority, however, is teaching the children how to read.

Are there published reading programs that use practices supported by the scientific research?

I have learned so much in a short time that I'm bordering on being overwhelmed. I just don't think I can analyze another reading program without losing my mind completely. Yet that's exactly what I need to do. I need to review the classroom approaches of all my local primary schools to find one that will serve my son's need during his second-grade year. What I desperately want is a cheat sheet for acceptable publishers of reading instruction.

While it would be great if we could give parents a list of recommended published reading programs, this is not feasible because publishers change their reading programs often and our list would be inaccurate before this book goes to print. In addition, good reading instruction is dependent not solely on the instructional approach and materials but also on the effectiveness of the teacher. Important factors include the teacher's knowledge about how to teach reading, her command of language, her ability to develop a relationship with students, her classroom management techniques, and her ability to assess each child's unique needs and provide instruction to meet those needs. Ineffective teachers using reputable materials can bring poor results. That is why we are informing parents about what effective reading instruction looks like. It is up to you to visit the classroom and evaluate the reading instruction yourself.

We can tell you that the new guidelines adopted by the California State Board of Education compelled the major reading textbook publishers to revise extensively and improve their products. At this writing, Open Court Reading (McGraw-Hill) and SRA's Reading Mastery are two research-based, complete programs for classroom use with all necessary components. By the fall of 2001, however, the products of other companies submitted to California for adoption should be well designed, including those of Houghton Mifflin, Macmillan, Harcourt Brace, and perhaps others.

Several companies have produced more limited but effective materials for specific grades or for the decoding aspects of instruction, including Read Well, Sing Spell Read and Write, Saxon Phonics, Land of the Letter People, Alphaphonics, and Discovering Intensive Phonics.

What does scientific evidence say about the most effective approaches to teach children who are having difficulty with learning to read?

Effective instruction for students with reading disabilities includes the same components recommended for the general education classroom. Remedial programs differ from "mainstream" programs, however, in the extent to which phonology and language structure are explicitly taught, the amount of practice provided in the transfer of these skills to reading, and use of the attention-enhancing techniques that are referred to as multisensory techniques. Beginners who have problems with phonemic awareness and thus are at risk for developing reading problems in the future, as well as older disabled readers who have already developed reading problems, are known to benefit from direct teaching of speech sound awareness. The National Reading Panel found that phonics instruction significantly improves the reading performance of first-grade poor readers.[2] The subgroup report provided guidance on this topic:

> The conclusion drawn from these findings is that systematic phonics instruction is significantly more effective than non-phonics instruction in helping to prevent reading difficulties among at risk students and in helping to remediate reading difficulties in disabled readers. . . . Growth in reading comprehension is also boosted by systematic phonics instruction for younger students and reading disabled students.[3]

The International Dyslexia Association publishes a booklet about the type of instruction the association recommends for children with dyslexia. The recommendations are based on the consensus of thousands of educational therapists over fifty years. Several readable pamphlets summarize these instructional techniques, including *Reading, Writing and Spelling: The Multisensory Structured Language Approach* (the R Book). In addition, the International Multisensory Structured Language Education Council (IMSLEC), a consortium that accredits training programs for teachers, supports the following principles of instruction:

Overview of Structured Language Approaches[4]

What Is Taught	Description of Content and Method
Phonology/ phonological awareness	• Student learns that a spoken word is made up of individual sounds and learns to identify those sounds. • Reading and spelling lessons include exercises to identify, segment, blend, and manipulate phonemes. • Student learns how sounds affect each other in words, depending on their location and the influences of the surrounding sounds.
Phoneme/grapheme correspondence	• Student learns the association between the sounds (phonemes) in the English language and the letters (graphemes) that represent them. • Phoneme-grapheme correspondence is taught and mastered in two directions: sound to letter, and letter to sound. • Student masters the blending of sounds and letters into words, as well as the spelling of words by sound.
Fluency in word recognition	• Student learns to recognize whole words accurately and quickly through speed drills, decodable text reading, and easy text reading.

cont.

Syllable instruction/ morphology	• Student achieves satisfactory fluency in passage reading through repeated readings if necessary.
	• Student not only learns sounds (phonics) but also learns syllables and meaningful word parts (morphemes).
	• Syllable types and morphemes are taught for reading, spelling, meaning, and usage.
	• Syllable division rules are directly taught and practiced.
	• First Anglo-Saxon, then Latin, then Greek layers of English are the focus of word study.
Syntax and grammar	• Student learns facility with sentence structure through sentence paraphrasing, combining, elaboration, transformation, and reorganization.
	• Student learns parts of speech and conventions of usage.
Semantics/ vocabulary	• Instruction includes comprehension of language at the word, phrase, and sentence levels. (Semantics is that aspect of language concerned with the meaning of words, phrases, and sentences.)
Text comprehension	• Student reads and listens to quality literature, both narrative and expository.
	• Student learns to use graphs, charts,

cont.

and models of meaning; to ask questions; to summarize; and to monitor his own comprehension.

Principles of Instruction

Simultaneous, multisensory

- Teaching actively involves listening, speaking, reading, and writing in order to enhance learning and memory; often visual, auditory, tactile, and kinesthetic senses are engaged simultaneously to reinforce associations.
- Student learns to see a letter, to form it correctly, and to pronounce its sound(s) accurately—all at the same time.
- Student learns the letter-sound correspondence in two directions: letter to sound, and sound to letter.
- Student learns mouth position as well as key words (m-*monkey*-/m/) for basic phonics.
- Students say a sentence aloud while writing it, or underline and say aloud the syllables while decoding a longer word.

Direct instruction

- Teacher must directly explain and demonstrate all skills and concepts to student with continuous student-teacher interaction.
- Inferential learning of any concept cannot be taken for granted.

cont.

| Systematic and cumulative instruction | • Teachers present reading and writing skills sequentially and cumulatively.
• Whenever student learns a new concept, it is integrated with concepts already mastered.
• Instruction must follow a logical order (simple to complex).
• The sequence begins with the easiest and most basic elements and progresses systematically to a more difficult level.
• Each step must be based on previously learned steps.
• Teaching starts with the easiest language concepts and reviews and reinforces them until the student masters them.
• Student must have ample and extended practice. Only then does the teacher move on to the next concept, presenting new tasks in a structured way, teaching small units in order of difficulty.
• Concepts already taught must be systematically reviewed to achieve mastery and automaticity. |
| Diagnostic teaching | • Teacher bases the teaching plan on careful and continuous assessment of the student's needs.

cont. |

Analytic and synthetic instruction	• Teacher must analyze and address student errors made within the scope and sequence of the concepts that have been directly taught.
	• Teaching linguistic principles should be both whole to part (analysis) and part to whole (synthesis).
	• The teacher works in both directions for all concepts, whether the student is learning to spell and decode words, or at a more complicated level, to put words together to write a meaningful sentence and pull them apart for comprehension.

Parents may hear two or more different terms used to describe this type of approach. It is referred to as MSL (multisensory structured language) or MSLE (multisensory structured language education) or just structured language teaching. For our purposes, assume that these terms refer to essentially the same approach. The most important thing to understand is that the principles embodied in these approaches have been found to be effective in teaching children with language and reading difficulties how to read.

Each approach teaches the components of a lesson in an integrated, cohesive way, including phonemic awareness, letter or letter-pattern recognition, sound-letter association, reading words accurately and quickly, spelling word patterns, reading sentences with known correspondences and sight words, listening to and reading text for comprehension, and vocabulary development. In addition, instruction includes sentence writing, grammar and usage, and composition. Multisensory methods—those that coordinate listening, speaking, reading, and writing—help develop letter-sound associations until they are learned at an automatic level. By using several senses simultaneously, such as the sense of touch (tactile/kinesthetic) while saying the sound (auditory) and seeing the letter (visual), the learner can overcome faulty symbol memory. Students might learn the sound-symbol relationships by saying the sounds while drawing letters in sand trays, or writing letters on a rough surface, or skywriting a letter in large, sweeping arm motions. They might learn about paragraph structure by building a three-dimensional mobile that shows main and subordinate ideas.

There are many multisensory structured language (MSL) approaches. The approaches vary according to whether they are designed for groups in the classroom or individuals, and whether the students are in the early, middle, or later grades. At this point, research has not progressed to where we can say definitively that any one of these methods is more powerful than the others.

The Orton-Gillingham approach is the "grandmother" language tutorial approach from which many others are derived. It was developed in the 1930s and 1940s by neurologist Samuel Orton and linguists June Orton and Anna Gillingham. Together, and with a handful of other colleagues, they developed a way of teaching the structure of letter-sound correspondences, using all the senses to reinforce associations. Since then, the Orton-Gillingham approach has been adapted, developed, modified, and updated by a number of institutes, agencies, and private practitioners. Here are the nine most common structured language approaches:

The Most Common Structured Language Approaches

Name of Approach	Unique Characteristics
Alphabetic Phonics www.sofdesign.com/ dyslexia 1-800-755-7344	• Considered an "organization and expansion" of the Orton-Gillingham approach. • Students are taught how to mark the sounds with symbols. • Developed at the Scottish Rite Hospital in Dallas.
LANGUAGE! (Sopris West) 1-800-547-6747 www.sopriswest.com	• Designed for middle school and high school students. • Teaches many language skills in parallel. • Publishes teacher guides, as well as student decodable books.
Lindamood-Bell Learning Processes LiPS (Lindamood Intensive Phonological Sequencing) Program 1-800-233-1819 www.lblp.com	• LiPS trains student to be sensitive to different speech sounds in words and nonwords. • Uses oral-motor articulatory feedback to identify speech sounds according to the position of the lips, teeth, and tongue in making the sound—i.e., lip poppers (p and b), tip tappers (t and d). cont.

- Offers other programs including Visualizing/Verbalizing (V/V), Seeing Stars, etc.
- Has over thirty clinics throughout the United States.

Orton-Gillingham Academy of Orton-Gillingham Practitioners and Educators
914-373-8919
www.ortonacademy.org

- Developed by Samuel Orton and Anna Gillingham in the 1930s and 1940s.
- Most likely the earliest multisensory structured sequential teaching of the letter-sound correspondences.
- Offers structured multisensory teaching of sounds, syllables, morphemes, and spelling patterns.

Project Read
1-800-450-0343
www.projectread.com

- A comprehensive research-based program for reading decoding, reading comprehension, and written expression.
- Designed for elementary and secondary regular classroom instruction, as well as special education.
- Instruction based on direct concept teaching and multisensory processing.
- Materials available that provide teachers with strategies to create learning experiences for students to apply and master concepts; also assessment of student skills.

cont.

Slingerland Institute for Literacy 425-453-1190 www.slingerland.org	• Designed for the classroom. • Slingerland Screening Tests are for early identification. • Introduces blending of phonemes through placing letters in pocket charts. • Emphasizes explicit teaching of handwriting.
Spalding Education International 602-866-7801 www.spalding.org	• Adopted Samuel Orton's method for both general and special education students. • Is similar to Orton-Gillingham but with a stronger handwriting component. • Has a strong theoretical foundation, which is explained in *Writing Road to Reading.* • Emphasizes the mental actions of comprehension and the direct teaching of composition.
Starting Over 212-769-2760	• Developed for the older student, including adults.
Wilson Language Training 1-800-782-3766 www.wilsonlanguage.com	• Originally designed for students in grades 5 and above, it has materials for younger students as well. • Emphasizes teaching six types of syllables.

cont.

- Uses a unique "sound tapping" system early in the program to help the student learn to differentiate the phonemes.
- Uses a simplified method of syllable division instead of the traditional slash marks between syllables.
- Includes extensive controlled text for practice of skills.
- Offers a program for use in schools.

We would also add that other approaches work very well for some children. Phono-Graphix is reported to be a very efficient way to teach children basic decoding, although it has not been researched independently of the people who developed it. Phyllis Fischer's Concept Phonics approach is well designed for small group and tutorial work in beginning reading, especially for second grade and up. Jane Greene's *LANGUAGE!* curriculum and the direct instruction model of Corrective Reading (SRA) have been successful with whole classes and smaller groups of adolescent poor readers. There are a number of instructional materials designed to teach decoding of longer words to older students, many of which are published by Educator's Publishing Service in Cambridge, Massachusetts, and by Sopris West in Longmont, Colorado.

How do I decide which approach is right for my child?

> I have a son who is in second grade and will be nine in August (we held him back in preschool). I believe he has dyslexia, although repeated testing has failed to give us this diagnosis. He is the oldest in his class and one of the poorest readers. He has been going to a Wilson-trained tutor since the beginning of first grade, and she has recommended the Fast ForWord program. I also have heard a lot of good things about the Lindamood-Bell program. Please let me know your opinion of these programs.

Many parents ask questions about which specific multisensory structured language (MSL) program may be best for their child. If your child is struggling with reading and shows the symptoms of dyslexia, the choice of program is important, but the expertise and training of the teacher are even more critical. An expert teacher can obtain results with any one of the structured language approaches. The overall principles and components of an MSL program may be the same, but the techniques may vary quite a bit from program to program. It is more important to focus on whether your child is making visible progress with reading and writing. You will be able to see improvement within three to six months of beginning a program if it is effective.

For children whose phonemic awareness is least developed, the Lindamood Phoneme Sequencing Program (LiPS) offers an especially intensive way to teach sensitivity to the sounds in words. The LiPS program teaches students to focus on how the speech sounds are formed and to compare carefully the forms of spoken words while they are learning print. Research studies that have compared the LiPS approach to others, however, have shown that while it is extremely effective with children who have poor phonological skills, other well-designed instructional approaches may achieve the same success. Again, the components and principles of instruction and the expertise of the teacher are the most important factors in outcomes.

It may seem awkward to question your child's prospective teacher, but remember that in other professions people expect that potential clients will ask about their credentials. It is not enough for educators to say that they use one or more structured language approaches to instruction; they should also have been adequately trained and supervised in the use of the approach and have references verifying their competence. Attendance at a two-day or even a two-hour workshop is sufficient to gain an overview of an approach; however, to be competent at using the approach, a teacher or therapist should have completed an internship under the supervision of a master teacher.

For example, the Wilson Language program requires a specified course of study to reach two different levels of certification. There is a distinction between basic certification (Level I) and advanced certification (Level II). In order to be certified at Level II, teachers must complete fifty hours of Wilson classroom instruction (a seminar for teachers) and one hundred hours of practical training under supervision (called practicum). Level II certification is required to train other teachers in the Wilson Language program.

A student teacher who lives too far from an instructor may

be partly supervised by videotape. Similar requirements are typical of teachers who are completing other IMSLEC-accredited certification programs. When educators say they have had training in one of these MSL approaches, you need to ask how many hours of practicum they have completed.

The parent quoted above asked about the Fast ForWord program. The original Fast ForWord program (now called Fast ForWord Language) is a computer-based language therapy program developed originally to treat children who have one very specific type of learning disability—early and severe language delay. Such children have serious difficulties in understanding and producing language as toddlers and preschoolers. The program uses the computer to generate speech sounds at a slower rate than normal and to stretch out the transitions between speech sounds, so that the child has more time to recognize the sounds in words. At the beginning of the training the child hears speech that is much slower than everyday speech, and as the child gives correct responses within the context of games, the computer automatically speeds up the presentation of speech. It also provides intensive practice in listening to language for comprehension.

This program has been available since around 1995, but many questions are still unanswered. It was first marketed before what is traditionally considered sufficient independently conducted, controlled studies were conducted to demonstrate whom it might work with, why it might work, or in what way. Many experts question the product's use with a broader group of students, a group that now includes children with dyslexia in addition to those with severe early language delays. Nevertheless, the company has marketed it aggressively to school systems and language therapists, claiming on the basis of studies conducted primarily by the program's authors that it is an effective treatment for a wide range of developmental learning disorders, including dyslexia.

An article about Fast ForWord was published in the Summer 2001 issue of *Perspectives*, the newsletter of the International Dyslexia Association. The theme of this newsletter issue was controversial therapies. The issue editor defines controversial approaches to therapy as those that meet the following criteria:

- The approach is proposed to the public before any research is available or before preliminary research has been replicated.
- The proposed approach goes beyond what research data supports, or
- The approach is used in an isolated way when a "multimodal assessment and treatment approach is needed."

Dr. Paul Macaruso and Dr. Pam Hook, the authors of the article about Fast ForWord, consider Fast ForWord controversial because of the lack of published research confirming the benefit of the Fast ForWord Language program for improving reading (or spoken language) skills of children with dyslexia. In this article, Drs. Macaruso and Hook describe a recent study they and colleagues conducted in which they concluded that participation in the Fast ForWord program "did not lead to any advantages in reading and spoken language compared to children receiving similar kinds of reading instruction without Fast ForWord." A group that received Orton-Gillingham tutoring actually made more progress in reading, and the gains were maintained over two years. The authors also state that more research is needed on Scientific Learning's newer product, Fast ForWord Language to Reading.[5]

Children are asked to use this computer program for about four hours per day for sometimes eight consecutive weeks, and the cost is very high—several thousand dollars. Parents should always be cautious about embarking on a treatment that is costly and time-intensive for your child. You should be all the more cautious when there is no independent verification that it is an effective treatment, and until research confirms exactly which children (if any) benefit from an approach.

My child's school offers Reading Recovery to the lowest-performing readers. Is this a good program for a child with reading difficulties?

I have felt for a long time that Reading Recovery is not an appropriate program for LD children, and since our special education teacher uses it to teach all LD children, I see the results when they arrive in my third-grade class. I am not impressed. Also, many of our teachers are at odds over how to teach reading. Some teachers cringe at the word "phonics," while others are well aware of the NICHD research and the importance of phonological awareness, etc. Do you come across this very often? Is there a solution to this problem?

This third-grade teacher is justifiably concerned about the use of Reading Recovery (RR), as reliable research indicates that it is not the best approach for helping children with phonologically based reading problems. Reading Recovery is a first-grade tutorial program developed from the work of Marie Clay in New Zealand during the mid-1970s. The program was intended to prevent serious reading failure by identifying the lowest 10 to 20 percent of the readers in a first-grade class, and then offering them one-on-one instruction by a highly trained tutor for thirty minutes a day for about twelve weeks. For a variety of reasons, including aggressive promotion by its parent institute in Ohio, it has become popular in the United States.

According to the National Reading Panel report, a typical lesson in Reading Recovery includes:

- Rereading two familiar books.
- Reading the previous day's new book.
- Practicing letter identification.
- Writing a story by analyzing sounds in words.
- Reassembling the words of a cut-up story or sentence.
- Reading a new book.

The lesson design in Reading Recovery is structured, includes routines, and emphasizes the purposes for "real" reading. These are all necessary and worthwhile components. So what is wrong with the approach?

What RR lacks is explicit and systematic instruction in phonemic awareness and phonics. The approach to phonics is implicit and opportunistic rather than sequential and systematic. The teacher teaches sound-letter correspondence as the need arises from reading and when the child has trouble reading certain words. The teacher is also instructed to ask the child to use context to guess at a word that is unknown. A more research-based systematic approach, in contrast, would teach a predetermined sequence of sound-letter correspondences and would use decodable books designed to give practice with skills that have been taught.

In Reading Recovery the children read small books, called "leveled" readers, in which phonic correspondences are not to our minds adequately controlled or sequenced. But because RR teachers are taught to encourage children to use picture and context clues if decoding strategies fail, and to use books with words that cannot be easily decoded, students may receive mixed messages about how to approach unknown words. They may develop a bad habit of guessing that is hard for the next teacher to break. The program is fundamentally based on many of the principles of whole language. Despite the enormous quantity of scientifically based research about the need to teach phonemic awareness and phonics in a systematic and sequential manner, this program has not incorporated these needed instructional components. We believe that there are other approaches that are preferable for a child who is struggling with reading and therefore we don't recommend this program for your child.

Reading Recovery is a dominant approach in some areas of the country in spite of the unfavorable reviews it has been given by independent reading researchers. Independent studies have been unable to verify the success rates claimed by the Reading Recovery Institute's own reports.[6] Critics, such as Dr. Bonnie Grossen from the University of Oregon and others, often point out that the parent institute's statistics on success rates reflect the number of children who have successfully completed the program, but say nothing about the fate of children who were dropped from the program because they were not learning well, or the number who were never admitted into the program because their problems were too severe.

Many educators criticize the high per-pupil cost of Reading Recovery, which requires individual instruction and costly professional development for RR teachers. In fact, some estimates show that the cost of this intervention per student can exceed the amount spent on the average student for the entire school year.[7] Many researchers believe that the public would be better served if the funds were spent on professional development to improve reading instruction in the regular classroom, thereby reducing the need for costly remedial instruction.

The National Reading Panel's subgroup on phonics summarized the studies of three independent researchers that concluded that Reading Recovery should be modified in order to improve its effectiveness for more children. A group of New Zealand researchers, with financial backing from the New Zealand Ministry of Education, determined that the typical Reading Recovery lesson plan should be altered to include systematic, explicit work in phonemic awareness and sound-letter decoding. The modified approach has consistently resulted in higher and more lasting achievement gains for those children who are below average in reading.[8]

One parent whose child was provided with Reading Recovery wrote us a message about her child's confusion:

My first grader is having difficulty in learning to read. My husband and I considered getting him a tutor but decided against it, since his teacher seemed so optimistic about his learning potential. Consequently, we decided to monitor his progress carefully. Things seemed to be going fine for the first few weeks. I grew concerned, however, when I noticed that he was guessing at words and relying on pictures for clues to figure out words. He would attempt to sound words out occasionally, but without the success you would expect from a child who has been in school for nearly three months. When I tried to work with him and encourage him to sound out words, he would get frustrated and refuse to talk about it. I became concerned and more confused because I know that his [classroom] teacher uses systematic phonics, and she coaches her students to decode authentic text. Finally, he began to open up to me about his reading, and a complete 10,000-piece, 3-D puzzle fell into place. To make a long story short, I found out—completely by accident—that since nearly the beginning of school, he has been pulled out of the regular classroom four days a week to attend a Title 1 reading group. No one from his school has ever mentioned it or asked for my consent, much less my opinion on the matter. Additionally, the teaching method being used is Reading Recovery. When I read up on the program, I figured out why the guessing game was a usual tactic for him in reading unfamiliar text. Now it seems that he is so confused by the conflicting methods he has been exposed to, he doesn't know where to begin when trying to decode the simplest words—especially if there are no illustrations. Additionally, his self-esteem is very low, since he is aware that he is "a low one, and the rest of the kids are high ones," as he puts it. This is something that he was embarrassed to tell me—and, as far as I'm concerned, he shouldn't have had to. I feel that the whole Reading Recovery ordeal has caused damage that may take a long time to repair. I'm angry that I wasn't notified that my child was in a Title 1 program, especially since the methods used there do not meet with my approval. Now my son's problems include not only reading difficulty but confusion in approaches to reading, and low self-esteem.

We encourage all parents whose children are receiving any kind of special help through school to inquire about the approach used. Some Reading Recovery teachers are trained in other approaches and have successfully used the best of several. Some districts have adopted their own programs that go by other names, but are designed around the Reading Recovery lesson plan. You will need to ask specific questions and then be willing to observe your child receiving help if you do not feel confident of the answers. Most of all, you need to take your cues from your child: is he learning steadily, with confidence in his teacher's approach? The child's response to a program may be your best guide to its effectiveness.

chapter 8

The Older Child

My child is thirteen years old and in the seventh grade. He is doing much better after three years of private tutoring, but I am still very concerned. Looking at so much new data on the ways to test and help young children is fine and dandy, but what about these children that were not caught early and are still working their tails off to read? My son uses books on tape whenever he can, has a homework helper, gets outlines, uses computers, etc., but still he needs to learn to read better. How do we help the middle school and high school student?

This mother is exactly right. Her son uses accommodations such as books on tape and a homework helper, but he still needs to receive effective instruction in learning to read better. It may be very frustrating to learn about the importance of early intervention when that window of opportunity has passed for your child. Acting on behalf of your child, however, requires moving beyond frustration about the past and facing what needs to be done in the present. Rest assured that most older children *can* be helped and can catch up to grade level. More time, more effort, and greater intensity of instruction may be needed, as well as reorganization of a child's schedule, but it is never too late to do something about a language-based reading or writing problem.

Several recent studies have shown that older poor readers can be brought up to grade level and kept at grade level with one to two years of instruction.[1] Older poor readers have the same basic problems as younger poor readers and need to learn the same skills. Their problems, however, are complicated by years of frustration and failure. Many older students no longer believe that they can be helped. Furthermore, their problems with reading have become problems with language—especially of diminished vocabulary and lack of experience in using good reading strategies.

In addition to selecting an appropriate approach in instruction, you will need to pursue or select program accommodations. The most common accommodations for the older student are taping lectures, getting a peer note-taker, using a study buddy, getting extra instructions, extra time on assignments, or extra time on tests, demonstrating knowledge in a nonwritten format, and preferential seating. Accommodations, however, cannot take the place of effective instruction.

The process of helping a child through school may seem like a lifelong project to many families, but eventually all the hard work pays off. The fundamental language problem that caused the child to have difficulty in learning to read will also cause trouble with spelling, learning to write, learning a foreign language, and often in learning algebra. In addition to being alert for these potential challenges, parents should be equipped with an action plan for how to deal with them.

Why do some children do well in school for a few years and then begin to fail?

Our son had been on the honor roll for most of second and third grades, when his grades started to slip. We began asking why, but his teachers gave us answers like "He's not trying," "He's a lazy student," or "He's not applying himself." Unfortunately, because these were his teachers, we believed them, and our son continued to slip for the next two years. By sixth grade things were really bad; not only was he looking at summer school, but he was at risk for failing altogether.

Many educators who work with students with learning problems are familiar with two grades in which students often "hit the wall." Fourth and seventh grades are critical transition years when some students who were getting good grades suddenly seem to fall apart. Fourth grade requires new, more advanced and independent reading skills when students must all of a sudden read much more widely and fluently, and when the text they read is informational, such as magazines, textbooks, and reports. If students have learned basic decoding, they may get by in the primary grades without developing the fluency they need to support the reading requirements later. Many times the child who makes it through the early elementary grades without faltering too much has many other strengths that she brings to the reading process, such as a strong oral vocabulary, excellent analytical skills, and a good memory.

Inability to decode important content words is a major issue for these students once the reading becomes more demanding and more diverse. When fluency and independent decoding of longer words are necessary, the whole complex process of reading can unravel, leaving students overwhelmed and at a loss. In addition to being slow, they may not be secure in their ability to decode longer, multisyllabic words. Thus, as students read informational text with many new words, they may skip over or misread too many of the important content words and their comprehension suffers.

Vocabulary growth is a continual issue for children who struggle with reading. Research has shown that vocabulary growth occurs primarily from reading itself; only *some* words are learned through direct vocabulary instruction in the classroom. Between grades 3 and 7 a child's vocabulary generally doubles.[2] Children come to school typically knowing at least five thousand words. During the first three grades they learn at least one thousand new words per year and, by grade 4, are learning on average from one thousand to three thousand new words per year.[3] Growth in knowledge of three thousand new word meanings per year requires learning about eight new words per day. Reading itself is all-important because most word meanings are learned from the context in which they appear, and the language in books is much richer than the language of conversation. The teacher can only teach a few words every day that are central to the meaning of text studied in class. Vocabulary instruction in the middle school should emphasize the study of prefixes, suffixes, and Latin and Greek roots, as well as multiple exposures to words in context.[4]

Children who read slowly find it tedious. They are often not reading much at all outside of school because it is hard work and tiring. Most parents report that reading is the last thing the child wants to do, as expressed by this mother:

> My son is thirteen years of age and in the seventh grade. I spoke with his social studies teacher regarding my concern that my son does not seem to be a very good reader. She told me that he might have some auditory processing problems, as well as some reading difficulties. He gets all As and Bs on his report card, but I find that I must be on top of him to get him to start and complete homework, and he *never* wants to read. His reading is very slow and deliberate. Where do I start in helping him? I don't want him to get into high school and take a nose-dive.

When struggling readers avoid reading because they don't like it, they have much less exposure to vocabulary, sentence structure, and text organization than their peers who read well. Their spelling and writing typically suffer as well. One way of thinking about the quantity of reading that a struggling older student misses is to look at some research about the number of words read in a year by fifth-grade students. In one study the top 10 percent of readers were reading about 2.3 million words per year, while the children in the lowest 20 percent were reading below 134,000 words per year.[5] There is really no way to make up this staggering difference, but many of the strategies suggested in this chapter will help narrow the gap.

What are some characteristics of effective instruction for the older student who can't read?

An older poor reader who lacks basic awareness of speech sounds cannot learn to read unless this problem is addressed. Many students must begin with phonological awareness, followed by sound-letter correspondences. There is no short-cut to decoding words fluently and accurately, and no way to bypass this stage of learning to read. The programs that are effective teach all levels of language processing in parallel, but use techniques and methods that older students will enjoy.

Skipping basic skills is a mistake, just as ignoring the fail-ure the student has experienced is a mistake. Older students must develop confidence that a different approach will succeed when others have failed in the past, and that it's worth the in-vestment of their trust and energy. They have often given up on their own future. Other students or adults who learned to read late in life can often help motivate adolescents who are just starting on a serious intervention program. In addition, the use of adult-looking materials, mature terminology, and mature topics for discussion can help alleviate any sense that the work is "babyish." Nothing is more motivating than suc-cess, once students experience appropriate instruction.

Although the language concepts that are taught are essen-tially the same as with younger readers, there are some im-portant modifications for the older student. Sound-letter correspondence can be taught in the context of discussing six syllable types, rather than as single sounds one at a time. The Wilson Language approach and the *LANGUAGE!* curriculum move older students to multisyllabic words quickly instead of sticking to the simple consonant-vowel-consonant words that first graders typically read. The older student who has not read a great deal will enjoy discussion of serious questions that arise from shared reading. She may have the maturity to discuss genre, author's inference and voice, figures of speech, and text structure in a way that younger children cannot. Teachers must show students how to deal with the deeper meaning of text of middle and high school material and ask well-planned questions.

Older students have usually developed some bad habits that do not exist with the younger student who is just learning to read. One of these bad habits is relying on context and guessing to decode unknown words. Some teachers use nonwords so that students are forced to employ their newly learned skills to decode at a sound-by-sound level.

Instruction in study skills is important, including learning to read selectively and strategically. The older student needs to know that there are different strategies for reading. Sometimes it is appropriate to skim the text, whereas other times it is necessary to study the material by reading, rereading, and outlining. The student should read key parts of a book, ask the teacher for outlines to use in studying for tests, and work with study groups.

Most important, the instruction must be intense enough to narrow the gap between the struggling reader and her peers. The term "intensity" refers to the number of concepts taught, opportunities for student response, and opportunities to practice skills in meaningful work. Up to two hours daily may be needed in small group and individual instruction to bring a student to grade level. She must read as much as possible to gain the practice and exposure to text that she will need to catch up with her peers. In general, the larger the gap between the student's skills and her grade level, the more intense the intervention must be for her to catch up.

What can I do to help my child not lose out on all the content of her other subjects?

I have two daughters who each have learning issues. One is in fifth grade and the other is in fourth. My daughter who is going into sixth grade has been working with a private tutor for the last fifteen months and has made some progress. The tutor suggested that we take a break and see what happens. At what point do you stop the tutoring if you see minimal progress with your child and use alternative strategies like books on tape and using tape recorders in class instead of taking notes? Do you use college fund money for tutoring since the odds of going to college are not that great? Last year I read science and social science books aloud to each daughter to help with homework. Is this a good practice to continue?

Children who are not reading as well as their peers are missing out on lots of content. You may play a significant role in minimizing that disadvantage. One of the things you can do is read some of your child's work to her so that she will be able to participate in classroom discussions about the readings. Explore books on tape as well. Reading aloud, however, is never a replacement for the child being taught how to read herself.

What types of accommodations should I be asking for to help my child?

I have a twelve-year-old daughter who is dyslexic. She has been receiving remedial help from a certified learning disability instructor since third grade and has made significant progress. My concern is that in eighth grade she will be required to take a high school entrance exam. Do you know of any way that I can guarantee that special testing arrangements will be made for her?

Special testing arrangements are often made for students with a diagnosed learning disability. There are other accommodations that help the student gain as much as possible from the classroom curriculum. Some children listen to books on tape; most textbooks and literature are available through an organization called Recordings for the Blind and Dyslexic. Sometimes a peer can serve as a note-taker or a study buddy. Children can be allowed to demonstrate their knowledge of a subject through an alternative to taking a written test, such as designing a poster or recording an audiotape. Allowances can be made for spelling errors on work generated in class, and children can be granted proofreading help to correct a final draft.

Extended time can be helpful for taking standardized tests, including the SAT. If you believe that your child may need to take the SAT with an accommodation for a learning disability, it is wise to read the requirements well in advance. The current procedures require you not only to submit a diagnostic evaluation that was completed within the past three years but also to discuss whether your child has been receiving the requested accommodation at school on a regular basis. Check the Educational Testing Service's website for its policy or call for information (see Appendix 2).

It is imperative that accommodations are not seen as the method by which a reading problem is addressed. The child will continue to need systematic instruction in how to read, write, and study.

Why does my child have so much trouble with writing?

My son, who will enter fifth grade this fall, was recently tested and he was at the sixteenth percentile overall for reading. The special education services he received at school during all of fourth grade did not address his specific needs. His special education teacher often says he is doing much better than the other kids in the special education program. But they should be measuring him against the other fourth graders. In my opinion, there has been no systematic approach to teaching him the skills he needs, like basic spelling rules and English language rules.

Almost all children who struggle in learning to read also have trouble with writing even after they are doing well in reading. Two different aspects of writing may be involved, separately or together: (1) the mechanics of punctuation, spelling, and handwriting, and (2) composing and managing the writing process. Students who struggle with the writing process or spelling often write a simpler essay than if they were to express their thoughts orally. When a student has to focus so much attention on spelling and has difficulty with letter formation, the expression of ideas cannot command the attention it deserves. There is less room for contemplation of ideas, organization, and writer's voice. If a student is self-consciously using only words she knows how to spell, the expression of ideas will be stilted and uninteresting. Students should be encouraged to use a temporary spelling or ask for help with spelling when they are composing a draft. Many computer programs provide spelling correction.

Many children with learning disabilities fail to realize that writing is a process that involves several steps[6]. Often they need the most help with the first few steps: deciding on a topic, generating their ideas, and organizing them before writing. Sometimes these students benefit from being explicitly taught the steps of the writing process, just as they needed to be taught the skills of learning to read in an explicit manner. One curriculum that explicitly teaches students writing is called Framing Your Thoughts, distributed by Project Read. This curriculum starts by teaching children how to construct a good sentence with the help of a visual code for marking the functions of parts of a sentence. Students diagram sentences by making arm motions or moving color-coded Post-it notes on a laminated place mat. The Post-its contain symbols to indicate parts of speech, which the student moves while saying the words in the sentence. After mastering the writing of solid sentences, students move to paragraph development and composition. Project Read offers training courses for teachers to learn this classroom approach to teaching students how to write.

Another well-known authority on teaching written expression is Diana Hanbury King. Diana King bases her methods on years of experience in teaching dyslexic adolescents. She is author of several books with exercises for teachers to use in teaching typing and writing to older students, all of which are available through Educator's Publishing Service (see Appendix 2). A third approach is very structured but very effective— the Reasoning and Writing direct instruction methodology that has developed from the University of Oregon. This is marketed by SRA, along with the Corrective Reading, Morphographic Spelling, and Reading Mastery programs.

Is it true that many children who have reading difficulty also have trouble learning a foreign language?

The underlying cause of the child's difficulty in learning to read in English—difficulty in processing language structure—will also create problems in learning a second language. The issue is more prevalent than ever before, as not only are high school students nearly always required to study a foreign language, but more and more middle schools are adding foreign language courses to their curriculums.

If your child is college-bound, begin thinking about the foreign language issue before she enters high school. There are several strategies for her to consider:

- Take enough high school foreign language classes so that when taking the same language in college the student can keep up with the fast pace of the college course.
- Consider starting over at the beginning-level courses in college, and taking these courses pass/fail.

- Seek a foreign language waiver for high school and college.
  Some colleges allow students with documented learning
  disabilities to substitute courses such as the literature or
  history of other cultures.

It is important to think carefully about the decision to get
a waiver for high school foreign language, because it may have
an impact on college choices later. Some universities are not
as willing as others to waive the requirement. Many high
schools and colleges require evidence of having attempted a
foreign language and failed before granting a waiver.
However, students who don't fail may have spent an inordi-
nate amount of time to get an acceptable grade. Consider requesting a letter from instructors or tutors to document your
child's history of difficulty with second-language learning, or
the strategies or accommodations that were necessary for her
to be successful in the class. Always discuss the issue with the
college you are considering *before* enrolling, and write a letter
to confirm what was agreed upon in discussions with the ad-
missions officer. A helpful article to read on this topic is
"Foreign Language Learning and Learning Disabilities:
Making the College Transition," by Sally S. Scott and Elaine
Manglitz, published in the 2000 annual journal of the
National Center for Learning Disabilities, *Their World*.[7]

Why do some students with dyslexia have trouble in mathematics?

Although not all students with dyslexia have problems in
math, many do, especially in algebra. Many LD students
struggle with algebra because it shifts from the concrete

thinking of grade school arithmetic to the more abstract reasoning involved in solving multistep variable equations. So much about learning mathematics is dependent upon the instructor's language and the student's language that in order to learn math concepts, the student needs to discuss, question, and articulate what she has learned. To the extent that the student struggles with expressive language, she may have trouble describing abstract mathematical concepts using new mathematical terms. One common recommendation from educators who teach math to children with LD is to provide manipulative shapes that help make abstract mathematical concepts more concrete.

Solving word problems can also be challenging, because they require decoding, comprehension, sequencing, and understanding the mathematical concepts involved. Think about the importance of the placement and meaning of pronouns in word problems. Words such as *next, from, of, by, with,* and *all together* signal to the student exactly what operation and equation she needs to construct.

You can help your child by seeking accommodations that help her keep up with the curriculum content and by understanding the difficulties beyond learning to read. Although accommodations are useful, the most important thing is to assure that your child receives effective and intensive instruction that enables her to catch up in reading. It is critical for you to support and encourage your child to never give up on learning to read. Her whole future may well depend on it.

chapter 9

Navigating the IEP Process

It was obvious in the first grade that my son was having problems. The school has had him in special reading groups ever since. At the start of fourth grade he was tested independently by a tutor at a learning clinic and found to be reading on a second-grade level. After I hired a private tutor, who is using a multisensory structured phonics approach, my son is doing much better. I thank God I can afford the tutoring. I'm confident that I'm on the right road. I will never let up my vigilance for getting my boy what he needs. My biggest problem now is that I can't get his school to write an IEP with measurable goals and objectives. They want to rely on "teacher observation" to determine if my son is making any improvement. I've had six one-hour meetings with them and envision that my picture is on a dartboard in the teachers' lounge. At what point should I give up? I want an IEP that is legally correct and educationally useful, but at some point, will this conflict be taken out on my son?

 We know parents who have been very successful at getting excellent special education services for their child in public schools, but too often with effort, frustration, and fear such as expressed above. These parents were informed of their legal rights, informed about effective instruction, good at writing IEP goals that are measurable, and able to be persuasive in IEP meetings. The parents who have been successful at getting appropriate training for special education teachers so that effective instruction is delivered are actually blazing a trail not only for their own child but for others who follow behind. This chapter will provide an overview of that process. We trust you will consult Appendix 2 for more resources. In this chapter we provide:

- An overview of the IEP process.
- Guidance on when you need to hire an advocate.
- Information about how to write measurable IEP goals.
- Advice about writing a parent report, along with two sample formats.

What are the steps in an IEP process, and what is IDEA?

The term "Individualized Education Plan" (IEP) refers to both the meeting at which parents and school personnel jointly make decisions about an educational program for a child with a disability, and the written educational plan that is generated at the meeting. Generally, the IEP document also includes statements about supplementary services and who will pay for them and how the student's progress toward objectives will be determined.

The process begins when either a teacher or a parent recommends a student for evaluation. Once your child is referred for testing, you are entering a process governed by disability laws that prescribe many decision-making steps. The major federal law that governs the eligibility of students with learning disabilities to receive special services through their public school is called the Individuals with Disabilities Education Act, or IDEA (also known as Public Law 94-142—Education for All Handicapped Children Act—and commonly referred to as PL 94-142). After years of parent advocacy, Congress passed IDEA in 1975 because some public schools had turned away, mistreated, or ignored children with various types of disabilities claiming that they did not have the expertise, resources, or inclination to serve them. IDEA provides definitions, outlines procedures, and provides the regulations that public school systems must follow because they receive federal funding. The act itself and the case law interpretations of IDEA, as well as state supplements and extensions of IDEA, provide the guidelines that school districts use to determine which students are eligible for special education services.

There are four terms that parents need to become familiar with:

- FAPE, free and appropriate public education.
- FERPA, Family Educational Rights and Privacy Act.
- LRE, least restrictive environment.
- Due process.

IDEA entitles all children to receive a free and appropriate public education, known as FAPE. A key word here is "appropriate," which is left to interpretation and has been the subject of much litigation. FERPA is the act that gives parents the right of access to all school records on their child and the right to receive a copy of the records (some schools require parents to pay for copies). The act also provides regulations about the confidentiality of these records, requires the written consent of parents prior to disclosing information, and allows parents to "amend" records that are not representative of the child's current behavior. IDEA states that "to the maximum extent appropriate" children with disabilities should be educated in the "least restrictive environment" with children who do not have disabilities. The parents also have a right to challenge recommendations made by the school regarding their child's education; you have a right to due process as well as equal access to information.

The special education process is just that—a process. It proceeds from the point at which your child is referred for testing and continues for as long as he receives special education services, if he is found eligible. Here is an overview of this process:

1. *Referral for evaluation.* Parents, school personnel, a student, or others can make this request, which should be in writing. The parent will be asked to give written permission for an initial evaluation, but we recommend signing this form only when you fully understand your rights.

2. *Evaluation.* The school will complete an evaluation of your child by hiring an outside professional or by having a school psychologist deliver the tests individually, often over several sessions.

3. *Determination of eligibility for special education services.* Typically, a team of administrators, you, and the school psychologist will meet to review the test results and determine if your child is eligible to receive special education

services. If your child is not eligible, you will be notified and the process stops. However, you have a right to disagree with the results and also to request an independent educational evaluation to be conducted at the school's expense.

4. *Completion of an IEP.* The IEP is a written plan for your child's individualized education and is prepared by a team and discussed at a meeting where the child's present level of performance, unique needs, and annual goals are discussed. You are an equal participant at this meeting.

5. *Establishment of specific annual goals and objectives.* An important part of the IEP process is establishing goals for your child for the year. You need to make sure that you agree that these are the important goals and that they are measurable and specific, so that progress can be accurately assessed.

6. *Specification of services your child will receive.* The IEP states the type and duration of services to be delivered to your child. The services enumerated include accommodations such as receiving books on tape, having access to extra time for testing, and having access to a computer for writing projects.

7. *Determination of classroom placement.* The decision about where your child will be educated is spelled out, whether it is in the regular education classroom, the special education resource room for a specified number of minutes per day, a self-contained special education program for the entire day, or an off-campus program such as a residential school specializing in learning disabilities. IDEA specifies that your child must be placed in the least restrictive environment appropriate to your child's needs. Sometimes the placement de-

cision is made at the IEP meeting, and other times this occurs at a separate meeting, often referred to as a placement meeting.

8. **Reevaluation of goals periodically.** You will receive reports on your child's progress at least as often as parents of children without disabilities receive reports. In most cases there are several review meetings throughout the year to discuss the child's progress. IDEA also calls for children to be evaluated at least every three years to determine if they are still eligible for special services.

9. **Exercising your right to dispute.** If needed, there are steps you can take to dispute any aspect of the process or the IEP. There are two major avenues. Mediation involves an impartial person called a mediator who helps both sides reach an acceptable agreement without going to a hearing. A due process hearing is a trial-like proceeding in which the parents challenge the school's educational plans for their child and try to convince an independent hearing officer to make changes in the IEP, order reimbursement for costs they have incurred, or provide compensatory education.

To have any chance of success with due process, parents must hire either an attorney or a nonattorney advocate. Either side can also take legal actions in the courts if they continue to disagree with the outcome of a hearing.

What changes were made to IDEA when it was reauthorized in 1997?

In 1997 Congress changed some of the regulations of IDEA on the basis of research about the effectiveness of special education. There were three interesting findings that emerged from this research at that time:

- Special education services were often ineffective because of low expectations for the student's performance, and an insufficient focus on applying proven and research-based methods to teach children with learning disabilities.
- The role of parents in the IEP process needed to be strengthened.
- School districts needed incentives to intervene earlier instead of waiting for children to fail to perform before initiating special instruction.

The effectiveness of special education has been questioned for years. Many special educators and parents feel as if the IDEA created a kind of Gordian knot of legal complexity that actually works to the detriment of children. A concern frequently raised is that children with learning disabilities may be identified but may still not receive the type of intensive, specialized instruction they need. Because the caseloads of special education instructors have been too high and the disabilities they must deal with are too varied, services are often delivered in large groups or in resource room settings that are not conducive to learning. Often the instruction is determined by what the teacher knows, not what the individual student needs, and special education credentials do not require teachers to know any multisensory structured language approach. Too often IEP decisions are based on the delivery system in place or the category of disability rather than the child's individualized needs.[1] Ideally, the child's needs should determine what is done; actually, schools operate as organizations with limited resources that cannot serve every individual. It is illegal for a school district to say to a parent something like, "Johnny has a reading disability, and therefore we will send him to the resource room for forty-five minutes a day because that's what we do with children who have reading disabilities." Every child's IEP is *supposed* to be individualized.

In reality, special educators must find ways to write and monitor many IEPs and often resort to "boilerplate" IEP templates in order to make their jobs possible. The paperwork demands of the IEP process are so great for the public school special educator that many of our best teachers do not have time to actually teach children.

Many children with learning disabilities receive modifications and accommodations to academic requirements and practices in lieu of the instruction that will remediate their problems. For example, they may be given modified homework or no homework, help with organizing their notebooks in school, or proofreading assistance. The law actually emphasizes *access* to the general curriculum, not full integration into regular classes. With the increased emphasis on providing special education within the regular education classroom ("inclusion"), children's needs for specialized instruction are often not met. The classroom teacher can accommodate children in many ways, but usually cannot provide the specialized, intensive teaching that is necessary for many children with complex or significant problems. In addition, the regular classroom teacher's training and orientation require her to teach the majority of children in the class. She cannot be expected to have the same level of expertise as a specialist, nor can she be equally effective with all children.

Fortunately, the role of parents has been clarified and strengthened to ensure that parents are full members of the eligibility, IEP, and placement teams. The 1997 IDEA is more specific about all the participants at IEP meetings. Parents need to read the regulations on special education placement to make sure procedures are followed. There must be a person present who can interpret for the parents the instructional implications of the evaluation and the proposed IEP, and there must be a district representative who has the authority to spend money. Although the regular education teacher is a member of the team, she is not required to be at all meetings. Parents should ask two questions at the beginning of the meeting:

1. Who is the person who has the authority to allocate dollars to see that the IEP is implemented?
2. Who can interpret the educational implications of the evaluation and the IEP?

What does IDEA entitle a child to receive?

It is most important to understand that FAPE is an *appropriate* education, not necessarily the *best* education. As Dr. Barbara Bateman likes to say in her presentations, "FAPE guarantees a Ford, not a Cadillac." Defining the meaning of "appropriate" was one of the topics of the *Rowley* case decided by the Supreme Court. As Peter Wright, a special education lawyer, advises:

FAPE is not the best program nor is it a program that maximizes benefit or learning. Parents must never say they want what is "best" for the child. Children are not entitled to the "best" education. Reports from private sector experts should never say "The best program for Johnny is . . ." or "Ideally, Johnny should receive. . . ." If you use the word "best," this may ensure that Johnny will *not* receive this service or program. Use the term "appropriate" or "minimally appropriate" to describe the services Johnny needs.[2]

We advise parents to advocate for what they believe is best, but to use language carefully in describing what they want for their child. Many parents are successful at getting a good education for their child through the public school by being informed, clever, persuasive, and good advocates.

How does the school determine eligibility for special education services?

Most states use several criteria to determine if a child is eligible for special education. In essence, the child's test results must show a predetermined degree of problem severity, different in each state. In addition, the child's need for special education must be apparent. Other interventions should have been tried without sufficient success. Thus, if the child has a reading problem, he may be referred first to a non–special education intervention, such as remedial reading, before he can be a candidate for an IEP.

Most states continue to use a discrepancy criterion to determine special education eligibility for students with learning disabilities, even though this practice is drawing vigorous criticism from the research community, as discussed in Chapter 5. The discrepancy formula is *not* referred to in the federal legislation, and states are not allowed to determine eligibility solely on a discrepancy formula.

The practice of relying on a discrepancy formula is flawed in many respects, but we will name just a few. First, there is no evidence that children with IQ-achievement discrepancies require any different kind of instruction than children without discrepancies who also experience significant problems with reading and writing. Second, test scores are approximate, not perfect; they change over time, with different examiners and different circumstances. Third, a developmental learning disability should be defined by the expression of a set of symptoms, not simply by a low score in achievement. And fourth, the practice of documenting discrepancies encourages districts to wait until children fail badly before they do anything effective. There is no incentive to put resources into early intervention. When experts from the NICHD testify to Congress, they often advise against using discrepancy formulas to sort children into categories, but the practice not only continues, it is *the* prevalent practice in most states.

Is it true that the teaching approach, or methodology, cannot be specified in the IEP?

School districts have not been required to specify teaching methodologies in an IEP. Requirements on this very critical issue may be changing, however. During the public-comment period on the reauthorization of IDEA, the issue of methodology was raised. Parents expressed concern that they may invest a great deal of time and energy looking at the summaries of research on reading instruction, yet they may be prohibited from specifying the method to be used for special education services in the IEP. Attachment I to the reauthorization of IDEA regulations recognizes that although it would be overly prescriptive and an unnecessary burden for the IEP to include day-to-day teaching approaches (such as attaching lesson plans), there is a distinction between day-to-day lesson plans and the mode of instruction:

> Case law recognizes that instructional methodology can be an important consideration in the context of what constitutes an appropriate education for a child with a disability. At the same time, these courts have indicated that they will not substitute a parentally-preferred methodology for sound educational programs developed by school personnel in accordance with the procedural requirements of the IDEA to meet the educational needs of an individual child with a disability.
>
> In light of the legislative history and case law, it is clear that in developing an individualized education there are circumstances in which the particular teaching methodology that will be used is an integral part of what is "individualized" about a student's education and in those circumstances will need to be discussed at the IEP meeting and incorporated into the student's IEP. For example, for a child with a learning disability who has not learned to read using traditional instructional methods, an appropriate education may require some other instructional strategy. . . . In all cases, whether methodology would be addressed in an IEP would be an IEP team decision.[3]

Parents should emphasize that according to Attachment I, methodology is an IEP team decision, and not a district policy. The hearing officer may be more inclined to support the parent if the request is for a structured language program approved by IMSLEC rather than for a specific program such as Wilson, Orton-Gillingham, or Lindamood-Bell. At the very least, the program should be evidence-based: there should be solid research evidence that the program itself or the program components have been tested in rigorous, independent studies and found to be effective with children like the child in question.

The issue over whether the IEP can specify the methodology is one that causes parents a great deal of frustration. Typically, a parent invests hours of time and energy discovering the extensive body of research support on the effectiveness of intensive systematic structured language instruction. After having done so, the parent is not allowed to specify a teaching methodology in the IEP. Yet the parent knows well that methodology is critical to a child catching up in reading. The longer the school continues to waste time teaching with an approach that isn't working, the lower the child's chances of catching up, and the more frustrating the whole exercise can be.

How do you ensure that the school will deliver an evidence-based approach?

If you are able to specify in the IEP that your child will receive an MSL or evidence-based approach, you cannot ensure that it will be one of the programs recommended in this book. We must acknowledge as well that after this book was written, new and better programs may have been developed.

If the school offers a different approach, however, and your child does not show signs of progress after a reasonable interval, then your best course of action might be to provide your child with educational therapy over the summer using your preferred methodology and to document the child's progress. Make sure you have your child tested at the beginning and end of the summer, preferably using the same assessment tools that the school uses. You need to prove to the school or a hearing officer that your methodology produces significantly more progress toward the IEP goals than the district's approach.

Can I get the school to reimburse me for private tutoring expenses or private school tuition fees?

Schools reimburse parents for private program expenses if the district agrees that the school is not providing an appropriate education, or if a hearing officer directs the school to pay. Almost always the parent has to take the school district to a due process hearing to get reimbursed. Some parents do remove their child from public school for part of the day or for a specified time in order to arrange for special instruction. As we have discussed, time matters a great deal in how easily, well, and for how long a child will make progress in reading and writing. Keep in mind that if you ever plan to request reimbursement from your school district, you need to follow some procedural steps:

1. At the most recent IEP meeting before you withdraw your child, state your concerns and your intention to enroll your child in a private program at public expense.

2. Write a letter to the school at least ten business days prior to removal of your child, stating that you reject the school's proposed instruction. Then describe your concerns and state your intention to enroll your child in a private school at public expense.

3. If the school responds that it wants to evaluate your child, failing to make your child available for that evaluation may lessen your chances for full reimbursement.[4]

If you do not follow these procedures and you enter due process with the school district, the hearing officer is more likely to reduce or deny your reimbursement even if it is found that the public school did not offer a free, appropriate public education "in a timely manner." If you are serious about seeking reimbursement, hire a lawyer who specializes in special education law before you withdraw your child. If you refuse public school services before you can document that they did not result in sufficient progress, the hearing officer or judge will most likely ask why you did not give the school district a fair chance to prove that its approach was going to work.

You must understand that the burden of proof for whether a program works well enough is on the parents and that the odds of winning the case are against you. According to Dr. Barbara Bateman, an attorney and a specialist in learning disorders, school districts win 70 percent of these cases. The reason the school prevails so often is that (a) the student is usually making some progress, (b) the district has the right to choose the methodology, or (c) the district is required to provide the services in the least restrictive environment (LRE) and they argue that the parents' requests are excessive and in violation of the LRE provision of IDEA. Too many hearing officers and judges are sympathetic to these arguments because they do not understand that students with dyslexia and other learning disabilities can and should be expected to make excellent progress with appropriate instruction.[5]

How can I make a case that my child is not making enough progress with the school's approach to teaching him to read?

There is nothing you can do to make the school teach your child the way you would prefer. You have a right to submit information, fully participate in meetings, disagree with the school, and initiate a due process hearing. Probably the most important way for you to exercise your power in an IEP meeting is to make sure that the IEP goals are specific, quantifiable, and measurable, so that progress can be determined. If your child makes genuine progress, then you will most likely be happy no matter what approach the school uses. Even if you cannot force the school team to adopt a specific teaching approach, you can hold them to an acceptable annual level of progress toward well-chosen goals. That is why writing good IEP goals is so important.

In the book *Better IEP's* Dr. Bateman provides examples of IEP goals written so that they can be used to define and measure a child's level of progress in reading.[6] Based on Dr. Bateman's recommendations, here are a few examples of specific goals and objectives:

Example of IEP Goals and Objectives[7]

Present Level of Performance	Annual Goal and Objectives
Reads first-grade material at 20–30 words per minutes with 5–10 errors; guesses at unknown words.	*Annual Goal:* Will read third-grade material at 80–100 words per minute with 0–2 errors. *Objective 1:* By December 15 will read second-grade material at 40–60 wpm with 0–5 errors. *Objective 2:* By March 15 will read third-grade material at 50 wpm with 0–4 errors.
Scores 2.9 grade level on the XYZ Reading Test.	*Annual Goal:* Scores 4.3 grade level on the XYZ Reading Test. *Objective 1:* By December 1 scores 3.5 grade level on the XYZ Reading Test.
Spells words dictated from seventh-grade list with 50 percent correct.	*Annual Goal:* Spells words dictated from seventh-grade list with 90 percent correct. *Objective 1:* By December 1 spells words dictated from seventh-grade list with 75 percent correct.
Instantly and correctly recognizes/says 20 of the ABC Sight Word list.	*Annual Goal:* Instantly and correctly recognizes/says 120 of the ABC Sight Word list. *cont.*

Objective 1: By December 1 instantly and correctly recognizes/says 90 of the ABC Sight Word list.

Dr. Bateman also provides descriptions of services that are necessary for a program to work, such as "one-to-one tutoring in a multisensory structured systematic language approach; 5 sessions weekly; 45 minutes each; provided in a private, quiet area of the resource room."

What can I do to prepare for an IEP meeting?

The grade school that my eight-year-old daughter attends uses the whole-language approach to teach reading, and her teacher feels that, although she is at least one year behind, she is doing fine. She is classified LD, but the school gives her no one-on-one time with the special education teacher. I just hired a private tutor who looked over her IEP; apparently I could put it to better use lining birdcages.

Preparing for an IEP meeting means gathering a lot of information. First you need to request in writing copies of your child's entire file not only from his current public school but also from any preschool programs he attended. Many parents keep a binder with all records organized by date. You will need to review your state's special education regulations, your district's special education guide for parents, and the IDEA regulations (especially Appendix A). Before your first IEP meeting, get a blank copy of the school's IEP forms. In preparation for the placement meeting, and well before it, ask if you can have a copy of the IEP documents the school has prepared to discuss with you. Ask if you can tape-record the meeting; if the school agrees, then state the date and attendees at the beginning of the tape. Always take along a witness to take notes.

One helpful way to organize all your thoughts in preparation for an IEP meeting is to write a parent report. Once the report is written at the beginning of the year, it can be updated before each meeting. The report can take many different forms, but the general information is the same. A parent report typically includes:

- Observations about your child's present levels of performance.
- Comments about his strengths.
- Comments about his challenges.
- Suggestions about what you view to be his needs.
- Recommendations for goals and objectives.

In thinking about your child's present level of performance, think about your observations of him in all settings in and out of school. What do you do to help him be successful? The techniques you do at home offer insights about what works for your child. Do you keep a list of items for him to check off as he prepares for school in the morning? Organize his closet in a particular way? Make sure you establish eye contact to know that you have his attention before giving directions? Spend two to three hours a night going over homework he does not understand?

When you think about strengths, think about what your child enjoys doing and in what areas he excels. What skills underlie his interests, and how do these give insights about his core areas of competency? If your child loves playing strategy games on the computer and is a great chess player, describe these strengths as the ability to remember another player's moves and to employ strategic thinking. If your child can sit for hours while you read to him, mention the topics he loves and comment on his long attention span. If your child is patient and kind in teaching younger children in the neighborhood how to throw a football, note his great hand-eye coordination and his ability to develop rapport with younger children.

There are several important reasons to write a parent report. It helps you organize your thoughts before the meeting, and it becomes your written documentation of all your observations about your child. It becomes part of his school file and his legal record, should you have a disagreement with the school district. Less tangibly, it helps you gain a sense of control in the meeting because you will be well prepared.

Ask the school to attach your parent report to the IEP or put it under "assessments" in your child's file. Do not try to write like a professional unless you are one. Write the report in words that are meaningful to you. Some advocates who teach workshops for parents recommend that the report be similar to a letter, with section headings for the different topics. Other advocates suggest that using a grid format is more effective. An example of each follows.

Sample Parent Report[8]

Strengths	Challenges	Needs	Goals and Objectives
		READING	
• Is very motivated to learn to read	• Reading is so belabored and laborious that it impairs his enjoyment.	• To be able to decipher unknown words more quickly and with less effort.	Annual Goal: Will read third grade end-of-year material at 80–100 words per minute with 0–2 errors.
• Enjoys listening to books read aloud to him, both fiction and non-fiction.	• Reading level is 1.5 years behind grade level. He is reading mid-first-grade material at the beginning of third grade.	• To stop guessing at unknown words and begin sounding them out.	Objective #1: By November 15 will read mid-second-grade material at 40–60 wpm with 0–5 errors.
• Employs excellent memory to recognize 400–500 sight words.	• Has difficulty in decoding unknown words.	• To improve reading level so that he catches up to grade level by the end of this year.	Objective #2: By January 15 will read beginning-of-third-grade material at 40–60 wpm with 0–5 errors.
• Maintained a B average in language arts in spite of difficulty with reading.	• Has difficulty in completing book reports on time.	• To be taught to read using an intensive multisensory structured language instruction.	Objective #3: By March 15 will read mid-third-grade material at 80–100 wpm with 0–2 errors.
	• Has poor comprehension due to ineffective decoding skills.		

		• To have books on tape for science and social sciences, and other classes from time to time.	Objective #4: By May 30 will read end-of-third-grade material at 80–100 wpm with 0–2 errors.
		• Since September has received two hours a week of private tutoring from a tutor who uses the Orton-Gillingham approach (at parent's expense).	

SOCIAL

• Wants to fit in and have friends.	• Is not always accepted by his peers.	• To be placed in classes with his best friend, as much as possible.	1. Wait his turn in games.
	• Has trouble sharing.	• To develop self-control.	2. Share with others.
	• Does not always express his feelings in an acceptable manner.	• To understand how his behavior, actions, and manner affect others.	3. Ask permission to use other's property.
			4. Verbalize his feelings in a constructive way.

• Has difficulty in reading non-verbal cues, like signs of anger. • Does not handle teasing well. • Has trouble working his way into a game or group on the playground.	• To learn strategies for how to handle teasing in a more effective manner. • Help from lunchroom and recess supervisors in entering groups and games on playground.	5. Respond constructively to teasing. 6. Join a group with school social worker.

Sample Parent Report—Dialogue Format

Date: January of third grade

Present Level of Performance

Johnny is reading thirty words per minute with nine errors in beginning-second-grade reading material. Although he has made some progress, we are concerned that the rate of progress is not enough to meet his annual IEP goals this year. We asked the school for additional testing on September 20. The referral was not given to the special education department until late November. At the beginning of December we

cont.

paid for a private evaluation by a local psychologist who is on the referral list of the Illinois branch of the International Dyslexia Association. The psychologist diagnosed Johnny with a learning disability and specifically found that he is dyslexic. His phonological skills are very weak, as indicated by his 10 percent level on the Lindamood Auditory Conceptualization (LAC) Test and his 6 percent level on the Woodcock Reading Mastery Test Word Attack. Report is attached.

We are concerned because Johnny is still significantly behind his peers. We requested an IEP meeting on December 8 but were told that there were no meeting times available until after January 20. On December 15 he began tutoring with a private reading therapist who specializes in helping students with dyslexia. Because of our concern about his lack of progress and the district's inability to respond more quickly to our requests for testing and an IEP review, we are paying for this tutoring, which Johnny receives for two hours per week. The tutor we hired uses the Orton-Gillingham approach, which is a multisensory structured systematic language approach. The psychologist whom we hired to evaluate Johnny in December advised us that with Johnny's phonological deficits this is the approach that he needs in order to learn to read.

We work daily with Johnny at home. Each night we read to him for fifteen minutes and he reads to us for fifteen minutes. Each day we help him organize and complete his homework assignments. Sometimes we read the material to him so

cont.

that he can complete the assignment. Attached are two examples that demonstrate his strong comprehension skills when we read the material to him. We are hoping that over time he will need less and less of this kind of assistance. We talk with his special education and his homeroom teachers at least weekly to make sure that all his homework assignments have been turned in and to gather feedback about how things are going in the classroom. Johnny is not currently a behavior problem in the classroom, but we are concerned that because of his frustration with not being able to read well, he may begin to act out.

Strengths

Johnny has a large oral vocabulary, as evidenced from the 92 percent score on the Peabody Picture Vocabulary Test. He is highly motivated to learn to read and to do well in school. He enjoys listening to books read to him, especially nonfiction books about history or historical fiction. His excellent memory helps, because he has memorized about four hundred to five hundred sight words. He also has good analytical and background knowledge, so his comprehension is excellent once he can decipher the words on the page. He is doing very well in math, as seen from the grade of A on each of his report cards last year. He enjoys working with computers and is beginning to learn to type using a hunt-and-peck strategy at this point. He is good at sports and fits in well socially. His attention span is very long, especially when building struc-

cont.

tures with his Legos, which often occupies him for over an hour at a time.

Challenges

Johnny is struggling with decoding single words. His reading is so belabored that often he cannot remember what he has read once he reaches the end of a sentence. When he reaches an unknown word, he never begins to sound it out. Instead he looks at the pictures, skips the word and reads to the end of the sentence, or tries to guess from the initial consonant. This is causing him to miss a lot of the meaning of what he is reading. He doesn't seem to be able to sound out any part of unknown words except for the initial consonant sounds. When he writes words, he will either spell the word perfectly because it is one of the sight words he has memorized, or he will not come anywhere close to an accurate spelling. Often I cannot even guess what he is trying to write, because he leaves so many sounds out of the word. This is why I always ask him to read it to me. He is very embarrassed that he cannot read as well as his peers, and it is starting to have an impact on how he feels about coming to school each day. We are concerned that although he is not a behavior problem in the classroom now, this could become an issue in the future.

Concerns

We are concerned that Johnny is not making enough progress in reading, writing, and spelling. The private tutor-

cont.

ing we are providing is multisensory structured systematic phonics, and we would like the same approach to be provided to him during his special education resource room time. We would like to establish a goal that he will catch up to grade level by the end of this school year.

One of the most important things about preparing for an IEP meeting is to think about what you need to accomplish in the meeting and what attitude is likely to get you the results you want. As Brice Palmer, an advocate, likes to say in his presentations, "Develop a language of persuasion rather than a language of positional battle." It helps to start with this approach and maintain it for as long as it works.

How can I overcome my feelings of intimidation in IEP meetings?

Being an equal partner at the IEP meeting is not always easy for parents. Some parents feel they must defer to educators because they are the presumed experts on curriculum and instruction. I have observed IEP meetings in which educators use intimidating educational jargon. If this happens in an IEP meeting, parents should stop the meeting and ask for an explanation of what is being discussed. You are certain to lose your sense of full participation in the meeting if you allow people to talk about things that you do not know and understand. You will, however, need to meet the educators halfway by studying documents ahead of time or keeping a special (and ever growing!) vocabulary list of your own.

Recently, some parents invited me (Susan) to accompany them to their son's IEP meeting. I was surprised and dismayed at the principal's approach to the family. Her tone of voice and attitude made even me feel uncomfortable. The meeting occurred in September; it was the child's first IEP meeting of the new school year in which the parents intended to discuss his lack of progress. During the previous spring the mother had decided to reduce the amount of time that her child spent in the resource room because she did not believe that he was making progress in the program as designed. He had spent part of the summer in a reading program offered by the school district to help students who were a little behind. The mother had also enrolled him in a commercial learning center over the summer. Neither of these two programs led to much improvement in his reading skills, so she was requesting that he be tested further in order to determine what he needed to make more progress.

The principal was rude and impatient with the parents, irritated that the mother had elected to reduce her child's time in the resource room. The mother felt reprimanded, not supported or understood. It was difficult to understand what motivated the principal's behavior, although it was consistent with her abrupt and cold style of communication. The mother became conciliatory, explaining that she had had difficulty in school herself as a child and that she was simply trying to make good decisions for her son. She shared her confusion and ambivalence about what to do to help him. She should have been treated with compassion, but she was treated with contempt and anger.

As we were walking through the parking lot after that IEP meeting, the mother shared more about her own early struggles in school. She told me that she simply did not want her child to go through the pain that she had experienced as a child. She remembers her excitement in the beginning of second grade and her eagerness to see her friends on her arrival to her new class. During the morning of her first day of second grade someone came to her classroom and escorted her to the principal's office. She was told then that a decision had been made to send her back to first grade for a repeat year. She was devastated. She had come to school expecting to be a second grader with her friends; she went home that day surprised and embarrassed to find she was returned to first grade. Of course, this mother will relive these memories as she reenters school to advocate for her child. She will feel vulnerable and uncertain, and will project her own feelings and memories onto her son. She will also have little trust in school personnel or, for that matter, any school-based program. She was wise to invite an advocate to the meeting, and it was unfortunate that the principal could not see the meeting as an opportunity to reconsider all reasonable options.

What do I do if the school isn't following the IEP?

We have had many instances of the school not following the way the IEP was written. They were supposed to get our son a reader for his standardized test, the IOWA Test of Basic Skills, and they did not do it. I found out about it and raised a stink. The music teacher seems to think that she does not need to follow it. The IEP clearly states that he not be graded on spelling because he is dyslexic and that if he is phonetically close, he gets credit. Well, the music teacher failed him on two tests because of spelling. These appear to be little things, but they seem big to me.

The IEP is a legally binding commitment, and whenever you are aware that any teacher is not following it, you should document your concern in writing immediately. The school cannot vary from the IEP without amending the document.

What resources do you recommend to learn more about methodology and the IEP process?

The overview of the IEP process in this chapter is just that—an overview. You will need to do a lot more research to become informed enough to be an effective advocate for your child in an IEP meeting. You should also plan to contact a parent resource center in your state for free information and a schedule of parent workshops. These centers are created and funded by the U.S. Office of Civil Rights to help parents learn about this process. Some books and websites are provided in Appendix 2.

A Final Word of Encouragement

Equal participation in an IEP meeting, or in any aspect of your child's education, requires confidence in the importance of your parental role. You know your child better than anyone else, and you play a significant role in finding resources, figuring out what is needed, and observing signs of progress. The school cannot make good decisions without your perspective. One of the most important things for parents to realize is that they bring a very critical and special view to the table. The educators may know more about a specific test or a type of reading curriculum, but you know more about your child than anyone else who works with him. You are in the best position to pull all the information together in the best interests of your child. An evaluation decision, the search for help, or an IEP is your responsibility, too; you can and should be active, questioning, and involved. We hope this book will help you toward that goal.

Appendix 1

Assessment Tools to Identify K–2 Children at Risk for Reading Difficulty

Comprehensive Test of Phonological Processing (CTOPP), Richard K. Wagner, Joseph K. Torgesen, and Carol A. Rashotte, 1999	Pro-Ed 8700 Shoal Creek Blvd. Austin, TX 78757-6897 1-800-897-3202 www.proedinc.com	Test three skills: phonological awareness, phonological memory, and rapid naming. Subtests for five- and six-year-olds include phoneme elision, word blending, and matching the first and last sounds in a word. Also tests rapid naming of colors and objects, and memory for a string of digits and nonword sounds.
Fox in a Box, Marilyn Adams, 1999	CTB/McGraw-Hill 20 Ryan Ranch Rd. Monterey, CA 93940-5703 1-888-772-4543 www.sra4kids.com	Assessment and intervention kit for phonemic awareness, phonics, reading/oral expressiveness, and listening/writing expressiveness.
National Center for Learning Disabilities (NCLD)	National Center for Learning Disabilities 381 Park Ave., Suite 1420 New York, NY 10016 212-545-7510 www.getreadytoread. org or www.ld.org.	Early literacy screening tool available on-line for parents and caregivers to screen reading readiness of four- and five-year-old children.

cont.

Phonological Awareness Literacy Screening (PALS), created through the Virginia Early Intervention Reading Initiative	PALS 853 W. Main St. P.O. Box 800785 Charlottesville, VA 22908 888-882-7257 *http://curry.edschool. virginia.edu/curry/ centers/pals/*	Faculty from the University of Virginia's Curry School of Education created this assessment tool, which is available for a nominal per student fee by those outside of Virginia. Individual children's scores are tabulated with links to the activities on the Website that support any student deficits.
Phonological Awareness Test, Robertson and Salter, 1995	LinguiSystems 3100 4th Ave. East Moline, IL 61244 1-800-776-4332 *www.linguisystems.com*	Five measures of phonemic awareness: segmentation, isolation, deletion, substitution, and blending.
Test of Phonological Awareness (TOPA), Joseph K. Torgesen and Brian R. Bryant, 1994	Pro-Ed 8700 Shoal Creek Blvd. Austin, TX 78757–6897 1-800-897-3202 *www.proedinc.com*	Kindergarten and early elementary versions. In the kindergarten version the student identifies which of three words begins with the same sound as a stimulus word; also which of three words has a different initial sound than a stimulus word.
Test of Word Reading Efficiency (TOWRE), Joseph K. Torgesen, Richard K. Wagner, and Carol A. Rashotte, 1999	Pro-Ed 8700 Shoal Creek Blvd. Austin, TX 78757-6897 1-800-897-3202 *www.proedinc.com*	For first graders and above. There are two subtests: one measures the child's ability to read sight words, and the other is a test of

cont.

		phonemic decoding of nonsense words.
Texas Primary Reading Inventory (K–2)	Texas Education Agency Publications Dept. P.O. Box 13817 Austin, Texas 78711-3817 512-463-9744 *www.tea.state.tx.us*	Kit includes a teacher's guide, an intervention activities guide, magnetic board and set of magnetic letters, laminated story cards, and twenty-six student record sheets for K, 1, and 2 classrooms.
The Yopp-Singer Test of Phoneme Segmentation, Hallie Yopp, 1995	*Reading Journal* 49 (1995) (free)	This is a brief test that can be used for kindergarten students. The twenty-two items ask the child to pronounce a phoneme in words that vary from one to three phonemes in length.

Recommended Resources for Parents

Books and Websites That Describe Activities to Enhance Your Child's Phonemic Awareness Skills

Adams, Marilyn; B. Foorman; I. Lundberg; and T. Beeler. *Phonemic Awareness in Young Children*. Baltimore: Paul H. Brookes, 1998.	Activity book that describes phonemic awareness activities that can be used in class or at home. 1-800-638-3775 *www.pbrookes.com*
Blachman, Benita; E. Ball; R. Black; and D. Tangel. *Road to the Code: A Phonological Awareness Program for Young Children*. Baltimore: Paul H. Brookes, 2000.	Manual with forty-four lessons. Each lesson is an activity to develop phonemic awareness. Instructions make it easy to use at home or in a classroom. 1-800-638-3775 *www.pbrookes.com*
Fitzpatrick, Jo. *Phonemic Awareness: Playing with Sounds to Strengthen Beginning Reading Skills*. Creative Teaching Press, 1997.	This book is very parent-friendly. It begins with an overview of what phonemic awareness is and why and

cont.

	how it is taught. The activities are grouped by level of difficulty. Book includes everything you need, including picture cards, word lists, and alphabet cards. 1-800-444-4287
Oo-pples and Boo-noo-noos: Songs and Activities for Phonemic Awareness. Harcourt Brace.	This kit contains a book and cassette tape and costs approximately $25. 1-800-225-5424
Intervention Activities Guide: Kindergarten, First Grade, Second Grade. Texas Education Agency.	This spiral-bound guide is part of the Texas Primary Reading Inventory (TPRI) kit used to assess reading skills in K–2 classrooms. The guide contains activities to do with children who score low in phonemic awareness skills when assessed using the TPRI. 512-463-9744
Let's Listen: A Phonological Awareness Program for Young Children. Abrams and Company, Waterbury, Conn.	An affordable, well-sequenced handbook of classroom activities.

cont.

Scholastic Phoneme Awareness Kit and Interactive Phonics Readers. Scholastic Company, New York, N.Y.

Kit contains puppets, picture cards, games, rhymes, and activities. Phonics readers are computer-based.

PALS Activities
Phonological Awareness
Literacy Screening
PALS
853 W. Main St.
P.O. Box 800785
Charlottesville, VA 22908

Website developed by the University of Virginia containing activities to develop early literacy skills, including phonological awareness, alphabet recognition, letter sounds, spelling, and word recognition. A list of resources is included.
888-882-7257
http://curry.edschool.virginia.edu/activities/index.cfm

Resources That Provide Summaries of Reading Research

National Reading Panel. *Teaching Children to Read: An Evidence-Based Assessment of the Scientific Research Literature on Reading and Its Implications for Reading Instruction.*

National Institute of Child Health and Human Development, National Institutes of Health, 2000.
www.nationalreadingpanel.org
1-800-370-2943 for free copy of the forty-page summary and/or twenty-minute video.

Put Reading First: The Research Building Blocks for Teaching Children to Read	U.S. Department of Education & NICHD. Excellent publication for teachers based on the National Reading Panel's findings. 1-877-433-7827 or 1-800-370-2943 *www.nationalreadingpanel.org*
Put Reading First: Helping Your Child Learn to Read	U.S. Department of Education & NICHD. Companion publication 'for parents based on the National Reading Panel's findings. 1-877-433-7827 or 1-800-370-2943 *www.nationalreadingpanel.org*
Lyon, Dr. Reid. "Report on Learning Disabilities Research."	This article was adapted from testimony given by Dr. Lyon to a committee of the U.S. House of Representatives in July 1997. *www.ldonline.org/ld_indepth/ reading/nih_report.html*
Torgesen, Dr. Joseph K. "Catch Them Before They Fall:	*American Educator*, Spring/ Summer 1998. Excellent article

cont.

Identification and Assessment to Prevent Reading Failure in Young Children."

on how to identify reading probems early. *www.ldonline.org/ld_indepth/ reading/torgesen_catchthem. html*

American Federation of Teachers. "The Unique Power of Reading and How to Unleash It."

American Educator, Spring/ Summer 1998. This issue, which focused on early reading research, is excellent. Every single article is well done and easily understood by parents.

National Academy of Sciences. *Starting Out Right (Summary of Preventing Reading Difficulties in Young Children).*

Book with lots of background information. It contains some phonemic awareness activities and general information about what parents can do to help their child. Not as much on the research itself.

International Dyslexia Association. *Basic Facts Every Layperson Should Know; Basic Facts Every Professional Should Know* (Orton Emeritus Series).

Small booklets written for parents and the general public
1-800-ABC-D123
www.interdys.org

Resources about Learning Disabilities

Basic Facts about Dyslexia: What Every Layperson Ought to Know (Orton Emeritus Series, B Book, International Dyslexia Association). (Also P Book, *Phonological Awareness: A Critical Factor in Dyslexia,* and video, *Dyslexia: Finding the Answers.)*	This booklet, written by Angela Wilkins and Alice Garside, is easy to read and gives a brief overview about dyslexia. There is a companion pamphlet, *Basic Facts about Dyslexia, Part II: What Every Professional Should Know,* with somewhat more sophisticated information. 1-800-ABC-D123
Coordinated Campaign for Learning Disabilities (CCLD)	Website of the CCLD: *www.ldonline.org*
Ennis Cosby Foundation	Ennis's Gift Film—video about dyslexia. Moving biographical study of well-known dyslexic people. *www.hellofriend.org*
International Dyslexia Association	Free information packet about reading difficulties. For a list of tutors in your area, contact the branch nearest you. Consider attending a branch or national conference. 1-800-ABC-D123 *www.interdys.org* cont.

Learning Disabilities Association of America	Nonprofit organization with local and state affiliates that provide information to families and individuals with learning disabilities 412-341-1515 *www.ldanatl.org*
National Center for Learning Disabilities	Website includes an early childhood screening tool starting in mid-2001. 212-545-7510 *www.ld.org*
Schwab Foundation for Learning	Excellent website for parents *www.schwablearning.org*
Thompson, Sue. *The Source for Nonverbal Learning Disorders.* LinguiSystems, 1997.	This book gives a complete description of the characteristics of a child with a nonverbal learning disability, plus advice on how to help an NLD child. 1-800-776-4332 *www.linguisystems.com*
Torgesen, Joseph K. "Catch Them Before They Fall: Identification and Assessment	*American Educator,* spring/summer 1998. Wonderful article that is very easy to read. *cont.*

To Prevent Reading Failure in Young Children"	Talks about the logic to support the preventive model rather than the "wait to fail" model. Contains chart describing phonemic awareness measures. *www.ldonline.org/ld_indepth/ reading/torgesen_catchthem. html*

Resources about Testing

Greene, Jane Fell, and Louisa Cook Moats. "Testing: Critical Components in the Clinical Identification of Dyslexia" (Orton Emeritus Series, Book T, International Dyslexia Association).	Seventeen-page booklet gives an overview of the testing process, along with information about the skills that should be assessed in testing for dyslexia.
Woodrich, David L. *Children's Psychological Testing: A Guide for Nonpsychologists.* 3rd ed. Baltimore: Paul H. Brookes, 1997.	Book gives an overview of testing, how to interpret standardized test scores, and information about specific tests.
Wright, Peter W. D., and Pamela Darr Wright.	Terrific article about how to interpret test results, including *cont.*

"Understanding Tests and Measurements for the Parent and Advocate."	an explanation of composite scores, standard deviations, and means. *www.ldonline.org/ld_indepth/ assessment/tests_ measurements. html*

Resources on Diagnosis and Learning How to Learn

Mooney, Jonathan, and David Cole. *Learning Outside the Lines.* New York: Fireside, 2000.	Book written by two college students with learning disabilities who attended Ivy League schools. Tips include how to take notes and how to read for different purposes.
Olivier, Carolyn, and Rosemary Bowler. *Learning to Learn.* New York: Fireside, 1996.	Excellent book to help a student think about how she learns best.
Reiff, Henry B.; Paul J. Gerber; and Rick Ginsberg. *Exceeding Expectations: Successful Adults with Learning Disabilities.* Austin, Tex.: Pro-Ed, 1997.	Book written about a research project to interview seventy-one successful adults with LD. Focus is on their models for success.
Tod, Dorothy. *A Dyslexic Family Diary* (videotape).	A videotape that chronicles a mother's eighteen-year

Dorothy Tod Films
802-496-5280
dtod@together.net

struggle to help her son, who is bright and dyslexic, receive an education.

Resources on Topics Related to the Older Student

ACCOMMODATIONS

Educational Testing Service (ETS)	*www.ets.org/disability*	See the ETS website for a copy of the ETS Policy for Documentation of a Learning Disability in Adolescents and Adults. ETS administers many standardized tests such as the SAT.
Recordings for the Blind and Dyslexic	*www.rcbad.org*	Extensive library of books on tape, including most textbooks as well as literature required in school.

WRITTEN EXPRESSION

Articles on writing	*www.ldonline.org* Go to LD Indepth and then select the topic of writing.	Six articles on written expression and how to work with students with learning disabilities
King, Diana Hanbury. *Writing Skills 1 & 2, Writing Skills for the Adolescent.* Educator's Publishing Service, 1995.	1-800-225-5750 *www.epsbooks.com*	Series of books with exercises for teachers that help in teaching LD students to write.

Project Read Written Expression Curriculum	Language Circle Enterprises, Inc. P.O. Box 20631 Bloomington, MN 55420 1-800-450-0343 *www.projectread.com*	Written Expression Curriculum offers classroom teachers a structured approach to teaching students to write, starting with diagramming sentences in a multi-sensory way.
Henry, Marcia. *Words: Integrated Decoding and Spelling Instruction Based on Word Origin and Word Structure,* 1990, and, with Nancy Redding, *Patterns for Success in Reading and Spelling,* 1990.	Pro-Ed 8700 Shoal Creek Blvd. Austin, TX 78757–6897 *www.proed.com*	These two books are teacher's guides for teaching spelling and decoding in a multi-sensory format. Based on the Orton-Gillingham approach. Both contain detailed lesson plans. *Words* contains instruction on word origin by Latin, Greek, and Anglo-Saxon roots.

Resources on Advocacy and the IEP Process

Anderson, Winifred; Stephen Chitwood; and Deidre Hayden. *Negotiating the Special Education Maze: A Guide for Parents and Teachers.* 3rd ed. Woodbine House, 1997.	Overview of the special education process, what to expect, and how to prepare. Includes checklists and forms on how to collect data.

Bateman, Barbara D., and Mary Anne Linden. *Better IEP's: How to Develop Legally Correct and Educationally Useful Programs.* 3rd ed. Sopris West, 1998.	One of the best books on how to write IEPs. Provides an overview of the process, the law, work sheets, and examples of good IEPs.
Coordinated Campaign For Learning Disabilities	There are many articles on the IEP process and the law. Go to *www.ldonline.org.* From the main menu, go to LD Indepth. Then select IEPs and Legal and Legislative.
Council of Parent Attorneys and Advocates	Organization of attorneys and advocates who specialize in special ed. They sponsor conferences. You can order audiotapes from conference sessions through their website: *www.copaa.net*
Kerr, Sonja	An attorney who specializes in special education law. Located in Minneapolis, Minnesota. *www.kerrlaw.com.* Website link to Pacer Center.
Martin, Reed	An attorney who specializes in special education law. *cont.*

Extensive website with parent chat room.
www.reedmartin.com

Meyer, Roger. "How to Find and Use Professionals for Your Case: Shopping for and Working with a Special Education Lawyer or Advocate."

Four-page article includes questions to ask before hiring an attorney or advocate.
www.ldonline.org/lo_indepth/ legal_legislative/find_attorney. html

National Information Center for Children and Youth with Disabilities (NICHCY).

Many articles are available for free from the NICHCY, which is a resource center for parents.
P.O. Box 1492
Washington, D.C. 20013
1-800-695-0285
www.nichcy.org

Siegel, Lawrence M. *The Complete IEP Guide: How to Advocate for Your Special Ed Child.* Nolo, June 1999.

Very parent-friendly book that takes you through IEP process. Includes background on the process, sample letters, work sheets and progress charts, sample goals and objectives, and extensive resource list.

cont.

Wright, Peter W. D., and Pamela Darr Wright. *Wrightslaw: Special Education Law*. Harbor House Law Press, 1999.

This book reprints all the special education laws, along with helpful commentary on the law. To order the book: *www:harborhouselaw.com* or 877-529-4332. Authors have also published a Tactics and Strategy Manual. Visit their website at *www.wrightslaw.com*.

Notes

Chapter 1

1. Laura Rogers, "Poll Shows More Parents Aware of Learning Disabilities but Many Afraid to Act," news release, Coordinated Campaign for Learning Disabilities, April 2000.

Chapter 2

1. National Assessment of Educational Progress (NAEP). *http://nces.ed.gov/nationsreportcard/reading/*
2. For a description of a morning in an imaginary whole language and phonics first-grade classroom, see Susan L. Hall and Louisa C. Moats, *Straight Talk about Reading: How Parents Can Make a Difference during the Early Years* (Chicago, Ill.: Contemporary Books, 1999), pp. 86–88.
3. National Reading Panel, *Preventing Reading Difficulties in Young Children* and *Every Child Reading: An Action Plan of the Learning First Alliance. www.learningfirst.org/publications.html*
4. See Phil Gough, "The Beginning of Decoding," *Reading and Writing: An Interdisciplinary Journal* 5 (1993): 181–92.
5. National Reading Panel, *Teaching Children to Read: An Evidence-Based Assessment of the Scientific Research Literature on Reading and Its Implications for Reading Instruction,* Report of the Subgroups (Baltimore: National Institute of Child Health and Human Development, 2000), pp. 2–94, 95.
6. Ibid., p. 2–1.
7. Ibid., p. 7.
8. Ibid., Report of the Subgroups, pp. 2–84, 2–85.
9. Ibid., p. 2–84.

10. Ibid., p. 2–86.
11. Reid Lyon, "Report on Learning Disabilities Research," article adapted from testimony of Dr. Reid Lyon before the Committee on Education and the Workforce, U.S. House of Representatives, July 10, 1997, *http://www.ldonline.org/ld_in-depth/reading/nih_report/html,* p. 7.
12. Joseph K. Torgesen, "Catch Them Before They Fall: Identification and Assessment to Prevent Reading Failure in Young Children," *American Educator,* Spring/Summer 1998, pp. 32–39.
13. Lyon, "Report on Learning Disabilities Research," p. 8.

Chapter 3

1. Brice L. Palmer, "Basic Legal Research for Parents and Advocates," paper presented at the third annual conference of the Council of Parent Attorneys and Advocates, Houston, Tex., March 2000.

Chapter 4

1. S. E. Shaywitz, M. D. Escobar, B. A. Shaywitz, J. M. Fletcher, and R. Makuch, "Evidence That Dyslexia May Represent the Lower Tail of the Normal Distribution of Reading Ability," *New England Journal of Medicine* 326 (1992): 145–50.
2. S. E. Shaywitz, B. A. Shaywitz, J. M. Fletcher, and M. D. Escobar, "Prevalence of Reading Disability in Boys and Girls: Results of the Connecticut Longitudinal Study," *Journal of the American Medical Association* 264 (1990): 998–1002.
3. D. J. Francis, S. E. Shaywitz, K. K. Stuebing, B. A. Shaywitz, and J. M. Fletcher, "Developmental Lag versus Deficit Models of Reading Disability: A Longitudinal Individual Growth Curves Analysis," *Journal of Educational Psychology* 88 (1996): 3–17.
4. Connie Juel, "Learning to Read and Write: A Longitudinal Study of 54 Children from First through Fourth Grade," *Journal of Educational Psychology* 80 (1988): 437–47.

5. J. K. Torgesen, R. K. Wagner, C. A. Rashotte, A. W. Alexander, and T. Conway, "Preventative and Remedial Interventions for Children with Severe Reading Disabilities," *Learning Disabilities: A Multi-Disciplinary Journal* 8 (1997): 51–62.

6. Joseph K. Torgesen, "Catch Them Before They Fall: Identification and Assessment to Prevent Reading Failure in Young Children," *American Educator,* Spring/Summer 1998, p. 32.

7. "What a Decade of Research Tells Us about Learning Disabilities in Children and Adults," *NIFL Newsletter,* distributed in the *Roads to Learning* packet of the American Library Association, Chicago, 1997.

8. G. Reid Lyon, "Toward a Definition of Dyslexia," *Annals of Dyslexia* 45 (1995): 3–27.

9. Angela M. Wilkins and Alice H. Garside, *Basic Facts about Dyslexia: What Every Layperson Ought to Know,* Orton Emeritus Series, Book B, 2nd ed. (Baltimore: International Dyslexia Association, 1998).

10. Judith Birsh, *Multisensory Teaching of Basic Language Skills* (Baltimore: Paul H. Brookes, 1999).

11. G. Reid Lyon and Jack M. Fletcher, "Early Warning System," *Education Matters,* Summer 2001, p. 25 (available on-line at *www.edmatters.org*).

12. Gordon Sherman, "Developmental Dyslexia: What Everyone Should Know," *Newgrange Now* (newsletter of the Newgrange School), Spring 2001, pp. 6–7. Also available at *www.thenewgrange.org.*

13. C. Snow, M. S. Burns, and P. Griffin, eds., *Preventing Reading Difficulties in Young Children* (Washington, D.C.: National Academy Press, 1998), pp. 80–83.

14. Roper Starch Worldwide, Inc., poll, conducted for the Tremaine Foundation and the Coordinated Campaign for Learning Disabilities, 1999.

Chapter 5

1. Adapted from Jane Fell Greene and Louisa Cook Moats, *Testing: Critical Components in the Clinical Identification of Dyslexia,* Orton Emeritus Series (Baltimore: International Dyslexia Association, 1995), pp. 7–15.

Chapter 6

1. B. Foorman et al., "Early Interventions for Children with Reading Problems: Study Designs and Preliminary Findings," *Journal of Learning Disabilities* (in press).

Chapter 7

1. McGraw-Hill, publisher of *Open Court,* provides videotaped demonstration lessons such as this.
2. National Reading Panel, *Teaching Children to Read: An Evidence-Based Assessment of the Scientific Research Literature on Reading and Its Implications for Reading Instruction,* Report of the Subgroups, (Bethesda, MD: National Institute of Child Health and Human Development, 2000), p. 2–41.
3. Ibid., p. 2–86.
4. Helaine Schupack and Barbara A. Wilson, *Reading, Writing and Spelling: The Multisensory Structured Language Approach,* Orton Emeritus Series, Book R (Baltimore: International Dyslexia Association, 1997), pp. 7–13.
5. Paul Macaruso and Pamela E. Hook, "Auditory Processing: Evaluation of Fast ForWord for Children with Dyslexia," *Perspectives* (newsletter of the International Dyslexia Association), Summer 2001, pp. 5–8.
6. Bonnie Grossen and Gail Coulter, "Reading Recovery: An Evaluation of Benefits and Costs," research report (The Plains, Va.: National Right to Read Foundation, 1997).
7. Ibid., p. 24. See also James Chapman, William Tunmer, and Jane Prochnow, "Success in Reading Recovery Depends on the Development of Phonological Processing Skills," report to the Ministry of Education of New Zealand, August 1999.

8. National Reading Panel, *Teaching Children to Read,* p. 2–39.

Chapter 8

1. J. K. Torgesen, A. W. Alexander, R. K. Wagner, C. A. Rashotte, K. Voeller, and T. Conway, "Intensive Remedial Instruction for Children with Severe Reading Disabilities: Immediate and Long-Term Outcomes from Two Instructional Approaches," *Journal of Learning Disabilities* (in press).
2. J. R. Jenkins and R. Dixon, "Vocabulary Learning," *Contemporary Educational Psychology* 8 (1983): 237–60.
3. G. A. Miller, and P. M. Gildea, "How Children Learn Words," *Scientific American* 257, no. 3 (1987): 94–99.
4. Marcia K. Henry, "The Decoding/Spelling Continuum: Integrated Decoding and Spelling Instruction from Pre-School to Early Secondary School, *Dyslexia* 3, pp. 178–89.
5. R. C. Anderson, P. T. Wilson, and L. G. Fielding, "Growth in Reading and How Children Spend Their Time Outside of School," *Reading Research Quarterly* 23 (1988).
6. Stephen Isaacson and Mary M. Gleason, "Mechanical Obstacles to Writing: What Can Teachers Do to Help Students with Learning Problems?" *Learning Disabilities Research and Practice,* Council for Exceptional Children, 1997. Also available at *www.ldonline.org/ld_indepth/writing/isaacson_obstacles.html*.
7. Sally Scott and Elaine Manglitz, "Foreign Language Learning and Learning Disabilities: Making the College Transition," *Their World* (newsletter of the National Center for Learning Disabilities). Also available at *www.ldonline.org/ld indepth/ foreign lang/theirworld 2000.html*.

Chapter 9

1. These comments are based on a handout titled "Purpose of the IEP" for Barbara Bateman's keynote address, "Better IEPs: Remember the I," before the Illinois branch of the International Dyslexia Association, Oak Brook, Ill., October 19, 2000.

2. Peter Wright and Pamela Darr Wright, *Wrightslaw: Special Education Law* (Hartfield, Va.: Harbor House Law Press, 1999), p. 27.

3. Attachment I, Individuals with Disabilities Education Act, 1997, YE 34 CFR 300.26 Special Education; section 64 FR 12552.

4. Wright and Wright, *Wrightslaw*, p. 45.

5. Barbara Bateman, "Winning Services, Placements, and Reimbursements for Students with Dyslexia and Other Learning Disabilities," *Perspectives* (Baltimore: International Dyslexia Association), Winter 1998, pp. 22–24.

6. Barbara Bateman and Mary Anne Linden, *Better IEP's: How to Develop Legally Correct and Educationally Useful Programs,* 3rd ed. (Longmont, Colo.: Sopris West, 1998), pp. 104, 116.

7. Based on Bateman and Linden, *Better IEP's,* and handouts from Dr. Bateman's keynote address at the Illinois branch of the International Dyslexia Association's October 19, 2000, conference.

8. The format for this parent report was developed by Pat Howey, advocate in West Point, Indiana. Based on a presentation by Pat Howey at Learning Disabilities of America Conference, New York City, February 7, 2001. See website at *www.angelfire.com/in2/spedconsulting/index.html.*

Index

INDEX